Authentic
Learning

Authentic Learning

Real-World
Experiences
That Build
21st-Century
Skills

Todd Stanley

PRUFROCK PRESS INC.
WACO, TEXAS

Library of Congress Cataloging-in-Publication Data

Names: Stanley, Todd, author.
Title: Authentic learning : real-world experiences that build 21st-century
  skills / Todd Stanley.
Description: Waco, TX : Prufrock Press, Inc., [2018] | Includes
  bibliographical references.
Identifiers: LCCN 2018007947 (print) | LCCN 2018017106 (ebook) | ISBN
  9781618217622 (eBook) | ISBN 9781618217615 (pbk.)
Subjects: LCSH: Learning strategies.
Classification: LCC LB1066 (ebook) | LCC LB1066 .S73 2018 (print) | DDC
  370.15/23--dc23
LC record available at https://lccn.loc.gov/2018007947

Copyright ©2018, Prufrock Press Inc.

Edited by Katy McDowall

Cover and layout design by Allegra Denbo

ISBN-13: 978-1-61821-761-5

Printed in the United States of America.

At the time of this book's publication, all facts and figures cited are the most current available. All telephone numbers, addresses, and website URLs are accurate and active. All publications, organizations, websites, and other resources exist as described in the book, and all have been verified. The author and Prufrock Press Inc. make no warranty or guarantee concerning the information and materials given out by organizations or content found at websites, and we are not responsible for any changes that occur after this book's publication. If you find an error, please contact Prufrock Press Inc.

Prufrock Press Inc.
P.O. Box 8813
Waco, TX 76714-8813
Phone: (800) 998-2208
Fax: (800) 240-0333
http://www.prufrock.com

Table of Contents

Introduction

Education is what remains after one has forgotten
what one has learned in school.

—Anonymous

THE HISTORY OF AUTHENTIC LEARNING

All learning was once authentic. In the 14th century, when someone wanted to learn a trade, he entered into an apprenticeship where he spent several years with someone in the profession learning on the job. A book education was only for the very wealthy or the clergy. An apprentice would watch the master and then try to emulate what he was doing. Then, after getting the hang of it, he would be promoted to master himself and would take over the business or start his own. Thus, if you wanted to be a farmer, you did not go to farming school where you were shown charts and graphs or you took exams on how to be a farmer. If you wanted to learn to be a farmer, you farmed—same with blacksmiths, bakers, and tailors. You worked with someone from that profession, and if he wanted that trade to continue, he was obligated to show you the ropes.

Teachers go through their own apprenticeships. You no doubt spent time as a student teacher, watching the certified teacher and learning from him or her until eventually he or she let you take over the class. Afterward, once you found a job, you were given a class of your own and expected to do the job you once studied and shadowed. Doctors and electricians experience the same thing with residency programs and apprenticeships of their own.

In the early 1800s, public schools were created. This takes us back to the one-room schoolhouse. A single teacher taught all of the subject areas to a variety of ages. In this mutual instruction strategy, rather than just the teacher giving instructions, the older students may have assisted in teaching the younger ones. Next, the Mann reforms

Authentic Learning

came along, and children were placed into specific grades based on age. All of the 11-year-olds were placed in one class, and so on, and so forth. The major problem is this structure only works if all 11-year-olds think the same and have the same abilities. Any teacher who has spent any time in the classroom knows this is not the case. There are some 11-year-olds who are a couple of grade levels ahead in their thinking, while some 11-year-olds could stand to repeat some grades. This is the difference between what James Delisle (2006) called an *age-mate* and a *peer-mate*. An age-mate is someone who is the same age as you. Because of this, you typically share similar interests and can relate to one another, but not always. Peer-mates are something else completely. Peer-mates are those who share similar interests and relate to one another, but there might be a difference in age. Consider a 9-year-old who can have a conversation with an adult, or a 46-year-old who still talks like he is in high school. In a perfect world, age-mates and peer-mates are one and the same, and structuring schools like this makes sense, but we know this is not the way it actually works. If schools were authentic, we would place children in classes based on their peer-mates or their abilities, not birthdays.

Following the Mann reforms, we compartmentalized schools even further, not only breaking classes apart by age, but also by subject area. We specialized in content areas, such as reading, math, social studies, and science, giving separate evaluations in these areas and training teachers specific to these subjects. This is not the most authentic way to learn. Put yourself in a sociologist's shoes: Children go into one room and learn about one thing, then a bell goes off, and the kids herd themselves into another room to learn about something that has nothing to do with what they were just learning. And this repeats itself again and again the entire day, every day, for an entire year. How does this look in a sociologist's eyes? Without any knowledge of the school system, he or she would consider it some kind of Pavlovian experiment, where the subjects must turn their brains off at the sound of a bell only to have to turn them on again at the sound of another. Because we divide our classes up into these core content areas, we take the context out of learning. In the real world, you do not do math at work for an extended period of time and, with the blow of the whistle, switch to only using your reading skills. Instead, areas of learning are blended together, and you might be required to access math, reading, and science all at the same time.

More than a hundred years ago, John Dewey (yes, the very same library decimal guy) came up with a radical notion. What if schools were not just about learning knowledge? What if they were also a place to learn *how to live*? Rather than focusing on the content of the three Rs (reading, writing, and arithmetic), what if we helped a student to realize his or her full potential and the ability to learn something he or she can use later on in life? Essentially, Dewey proposed providing children with skills, not content, that allow them to be successful in whatever it is they want to do.

Consider the saying, "Give a man a fish, he eats for a single day; teach him to fish, and he will eat for the rest of his life." Ultimately, that leads us to the question: Are we teaching our students how to fish, or are we *giving* them the fish? In many cases, we are just giving them the fish in the form of content. We are not teaching them the skills needed to catch the fish themselves and survive in the world. The way we have positioned our school systems, we essentially attempt to teach students how to fish by looking at the different parts of a fishing pole and/or the various methods and equipment used to catch a fish. Students can recite these parts by memorization and identify the various types of fishing equipment by sight, but at no time do they actually go out and fish, nor do they experiment with various methods to find the one that works best for different situations. How enduring is that education going to be?

THE PROBLEM

When you think back to when you were earning your education degree, how practical were the classes that focused on educational theory, as opposed to those where you actually did something practical? We talk a lot about theory but do not spend enough time in the practice of these skills. For example, we spend a lot of time in social studies class telling students what it means to be good citizens of their community and various ways they can take part in it, citing specific examples. Would it not be more effective to have students work on their own community service projects where they experience firsthand what it means to be a good citizen and what it entails?

As you can see, the problem is that *our modern classrooms are often not authentic.* Students do not produce anything that is going to be used by someone else. They do not experience things for themselves and learn from that. The days of the few classes where students were learning a practical hands-on skill that they could apply to their everyday life, such as home economics or wood shop, are being abandoned so that we can get more math or reading time with students. School is an artificial learning environment. We are putting students in a vacuum and then expecting them to understand the context of where their learning fits into the real world.

HOW TO USE THIS BOOK

This book aims to provide teaching strategies that allow you to give your students an authentic learning experience they can apply to their lives. It will start with a justification for authentic learning and how it will help students achieve Domain D of the rigor/relevance chart created by the International Center for Leadership in Education (Jones, 2004), as well as how it teaches 21st-century skills. Each subsequent chapter will discuss a specific strategy, providing you with an explanation of the strategy and how it allows for authentic learning.

Figure 1 outlines the authentic learning strategies. It begins with inquiry-based learning at the top. All of the other strategies use a form of inquiry-based learning, so it is important to understand it. All strategies may use collaborative learning, so it is equally important to be purposeful in teaching students how to work together to achieve a task. Inquiry and collaboration lead to more specific strategies, which include project-based learning, problem-based learning, and case-based learning. Once you decide to use an authentic strategy, how do you become an authentic teacher? The book will conclude by providing specific tactics that can be used inside and outside the classroom to bring the real world to students and vice versa.

Authentic learning can be a very powerful way to educate students. It can change the way students learn as well as the way you teach. It will certainly create an enduring real-world understanding of what students are learning, rather than just surface-level memorization that will only benefit one if he or she is playing Trivial Pursuit. You can either employ all of the strategies provided in this book or focus on one and try to do it really well. The decision is yours, but by making this decision you are ensuring that your students will be getting a better education—one they will be able to use throughout their lives.

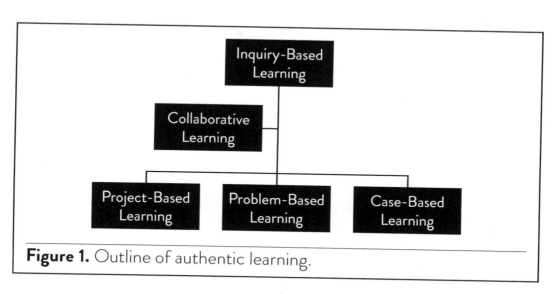

Figure 1. Outline of authentic learning.

Inquiry Based learning

↳ Students ask questions to discover the
truth
→ give pieces of information
guided inquiry — teaching step by step

Step 1 → Review rules of questions
  Ask as many questions as you can
 → change any statement to a question
 → write down every question exactly how
    its asked
 → do not stop to judge, discuss or answer
 any question

 → open ended closed ended

 → Star prioritzation
    question you want to further investigate
Step 6: what to do with the question
Reflect:
      ↳ use for research
    ↳ develop a
      project
    ↳ use the question as
      a guide

di active teaching - teacher tells them
everything - students

1 Chapter

What Is Authentic Learning?

[handwritten notes:]
real life scenario
students learn better with stories
storie has a scenario + problem → students apply anything they learned
– real life application

A. Explain connection between authentic learning and life skills

B. Discribe the importance of students reflecting on their learning

> Tell me and I forget. Teach me and I remember. Involve me and I learn.
>
> —Ben Franklin

C summarize an activity used in your teaching to get students to level 3 or 4 of Webb's Depth of knowledge

Simply put, authentic learning is real-life learning. It is more complicated than that, of course, but for the most part, that definition hits the proverbial nail on the head. There are many different ways to achieve authentic learning, but at its best, authentic learning should (Reeves, Herrington, & Oliver, 2002):

1. have real-world relevance;
2. be ill-defined, requiring students to define tasks and subtasks needed to complete the activity;
3. comprise complex tasks to be investigated by students over a sustained period of time;
4. provide the opportunity for students to examine the task from different perspectives, using a variety of resources;
5. provide the opportunity to collaborate;
6. provide the opportunity to reflect;
7. be able to be integrated and applied across different subject areas and lead beyond domain-specific contents;
8. be seamlessly integrated with assessment;

9. create polished products valuable in their own right rather than as a preparation for something else; and

10. allow competing solutions and a diversity of outcomes (p. 564).

Although all are necessary elements, there are a few that can be especially important for teaching students long-term skills:

Ill-defined tasks. Because the tasks are ill defined, students have to define the tasks themselves and determine what is needed to complete them. This leads to a very important lifelong skill known as *task prioritization*. Task prioritization is something that not only students could stand to learn, but many adults as well. Task prioritization helps prevent that dreaded P-word, *procrastination*. By creating a list of tasks and then determining which ones need to be done when, students not only learn how to fish, but also learn how to do so efficiently. Along with task prioritization comes *time management*. In learning this, students must choose how to manage their time. How much time do they need for each skill? What needs to be done first and by what date so they have enough time to finish the remaining tasks? They must manage their time the way that best suits their needs. What employer would not want someone who could prioritize tasks and manage time? What parent would not want that of his or her child? These skills will take one far in the adult world and will give someone an advantage over someone who does not possess them.

Polished products. Nobody likes busy work. And yet that is what students do a majority of the time in school. If they are lucky, an assignment might get hung on the fridge, or a parent might store it away in a memory box to pull out and look at years from now. Rarely are students creating something that can be used later or pointed to as an indicator of their ability. You would not take a test with an A+ on it and show it to a college recruiter. You would, however, take in a portfolio of your work that you created for a class or tell the recruiter about a campaign you worked on. If students feel there is value in a product other than just a grade, this adds to their motivation and produces higher quality work because they know someone other than the teacher might see it.

Opportunity to reflect. The best way to determine what someone has learned is not by having him or her complete a test or even create a product. The best way to determine what has been learned is through reflection. What a teacher wants a student to learn and what he or she actually learns can be two very different things. However, the lesson the student took from an assignment might be way more important to him or her than what the teacher intended.

What Is Authentic Learning?

For example, a student is working on a literary analysis paper for the book *For Whom the Bell Tolls* by Ernest Hemingway. The student receives a B- because the teacher determined he learned the basics of the themes she was focusing on, but he did not show a deep level of understanding. The student might have learned, however, that he needs to revise better. He understands the themes at a deeper level, just as the teacher wanted; however, he did not go back and compare his paper to the rubric. If he had, he might have realized he was not going into enough depth and would have added to his paper to make a higher quality product. His breadth of knowledge on Hemingway will not be of much use down the road. However, the lesson he learned of going back and revising his work will be a huge benefit later on.

The problem comes when the student does not reflect and come to the realization of what he actually has learned. What if he does not reflect upon the process and realize that the lack of revision was the reason for the B- paper? What if the student is content with a B- paper and goes on to make the same mistake later on, only at much higher stakes? We need to be more purposeful about allowing students to reflect on what they learned, not just assessing what we want them to learn. Authentic learning provides a space for reflection to occur.

BENEFITS OF AUTHENTIC LEARNING

There are many benefits of authentic learning, but here are six of the most impactful. Each benefit is important in its own right, but combined they make for a very powerful learning experience. Authentic learning offers (Windham, 2007):

- relevance,
- preparation,
- critical thinking,
- a multidisciplinary nature,
- evaluation, and
- interactivity.

Relevance

They say a picture is worth a thousand words. The image in Figure 2 sums up the importance of relevance quite nicely.

Authentic Learning

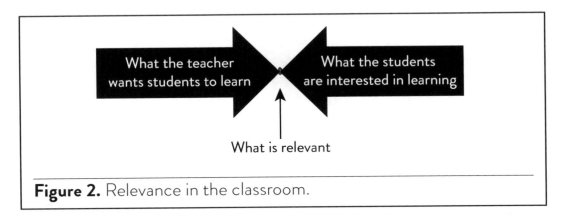

Figure 2. Relevance in the classroom.

Students often ask the age-old question, "Why are we learning this?" Just as often, the teacher does not have a compelling reason for this or will give the cursory answer of "because it is on the test." That is not acceptable. Students have the right to know the importance of what they are learning and how it fits into the fabric of their lives. Often, you will hear teachers complain, "These kids don't want to learn." Nothing could be further from the truth. These kids certainly want to learn. They spend countless hours of their free time learning about things that are interesting to them. They just do not want to learn what the teacher is teaching.

What if what the teacher wanted to teach and what the student wanted to learn intersected one another like in the picture? That is where relevance takes place. It makes it so much easier for the teacher to teach and for the student to learn when there is a common relevance.

An effective way to create this relevance is by focusing on skills rather than content. For example, in a junior high biology class, you might be teaching about hereditary and nonhereditary traits. In the past, students have completed a Punnett square worksheet to determine the dominant/recessive genes and the most likely traits a person will have. What if you made it more relevant by having students make their family tree going back three generations and follow the traits as they have been passed down? Suddenly, instead of just learning about Punnett squares, students are using them to learn about their own family history as well as how to conduct genealogy research. This is a topic that most likely will be of interest to them, as well as a skill that can be used later in life. They are learning about themselves as they are learning what you wanted them to. That is how you create relevance.

By creating relevance, you provide students with something they may not show a lot when it comes to their studies: motivation. A motivated person can accomplish so much more than an apathetic one. A motivated person will go places you did not even imagine, but an apathetic one will only go where you lead him or her. Creating motivation through the use of relevance can be a powerful method of teaching. It also makes learning authentic.

Preparation

Preparation is how ready one feels about tackling a particular task—whether it be cooking a meal or managing life after college. Preparation has a lot to do with confidence. The more confident you are, the more prepared you will feel. The best way to develop confidence is through practice. The more exposed one is to something or the more he or she practices it, the more prepared he or she is going to be when it arises in life.

An example of this is driving. When most people start out as drivers, they are very hesitant. This is why teens, those just learning to drive, are the highest risk group for an accident. For every mile driven, teens are four times as likely to be involved in a car crash (Autos.com Editor, 2013). The best way to learn to drive is not by reading about it, watching someone else, or analyzing characteristics of the best drivers in history. Authentic learning would have students actually driving. Exposing young students to experiences where they can drive in a safe environment will begin to build their confidence. As they become more confident, they will also feel better prepared when high-stakes situations arrive on the road, such as someone swerving into their lane or icy conditions.

Critical Thinking

Teachers should ensure every child leaves the classroom having the ability to think critically. Critical thinking is the difference between being educated and having an education. Educated people know a lot of things that other people do not. People with an education can learn about anything the educated person knows, as well as add to their abilities.

This will be talked about in more depth in the next chapter, but the simplest way to start students thinking critically is by asking two additional questions: How? Why? In the classroom, we are very adept at asking, who, what, where, and when? We ask these questions and then hunt and peck until we locate a student who is able to give us the correct answer. With questions like these, there is not much critical thinking happening. You either know the answer or you do not. When a student gives you the

correct answer, you should take him or her even deeper by asking, how or why? Here is an exchange between a teacher and student that demonstrates this:

Teacher: What is four minus two?

Johnny: Two.

Teacher: How did you get that answer, Johnny?

Johnny: What do you mean?

Teacher: I mean, what technique did you use to arrive at the answer of two?

Johnny: I subtracted.

Teacher: Why did you subtract?

Johnny: Because you told me to.

Teacher: I never said to subtract.

Johnny: Yes, you did.

Teacher: No, I said "minus." How did you arrive at the idea of subtracting?

Johnny: "Minus" means having a smaller number than I started with. In order to make that number smaller, I would have to subtract.

Teacher: Why not add?

Johnny: Because I would get the wrong answer.

Teacher: How would the answer be wrong?

Johnny: Because the number from adding would be greater than I started with, so I would not be minus-ing like you asked.

In this exchange, Johnny has to really think about why he chose the answer he did. It is not simply, "Give me the correct answer, and I will reward you with praise." Instead, the teacher effectively says, "I want you to understand how you got this answer."

Thinking critically leads to the following skills (SkillsYouNeed.com, 2011–2017):

- understanding the links between ideas;
- recognizing, building, and appraising arguments;
- approaching problems in a consistent and systematic way;
- reflecting on the justification of their own assumptions, beliefs, and values;
- identifying inconsistencies and errors in reasoning; and
- determining the importance and relevance of arguments and ideas (para. 6).

This all boils down to students being able to think for themselves. In real life, if you do not think for yourself, someone else will do it for you.

What Is Authentic Learning?

Multidisciplinary Approach

Authentic learning lends itself to a multidisciplinary approach. By working on an assignment across subject areas, students can see and understand the context of the skill they are learning. Being multidisciplinary is not reading just in language arts class and doing arithmetic problems just in math class. It is using whatever skills are needed to complete the assignment and understanding how they work together to provide the solution—no matter the content area.

Any modern-day invention is a combination of multidisciplinary skills. In order to create a laptop, someone has to develop the initial idea. Then, it is turned over to engineers who actually have to figure out how to turn the idea into a product. Several different types of engineers might be employed because there are so many aspects of a computer, including software and hardware. Industrial designers become involved in determining how to make the computer visually appealing. Marketing and advertising professionals likely generate web, print, and multimedia campaigns for the device, so that it may be sold to other companies and consumers. Finally, in order to mass-produce the device, workers need to craft all of the various parts and assemble the devices. At every step, there are very different skills being used by very different people. Without the combination of them, however, that laptop is not a success. When you break these various tasks down you cover many of the subject areas we break apart in schools, such as engineering (math), industrial design (science), and marketing (reading, writing, and communication).

The synergy of these subjects working together gives you a big picture of how they fit together into one product. We should be doing the same thing in our schools. Multidisciplinary approaches have been given a boost by the STEM (science, technology, engineering, and math) movement, as students participate in design challenges that incorporate all of these aspects rather than going to science class for one aspect and math for another.

Evaluation

Authentic learning is not typically evaluated using traditional methods of assessment. Instead of a pencil-to-paper test, authentic learning often results in a tangible product. The challenge—for teachers and students—is that a tangible product does not have a right or wrong answer. How many times in your adult life have you had to take a pencil-to-paper test to prove your worth? Most of the things we are evaluated on

Authentic Learning

are the tangible products we create, whether that is how well we manicure our lawn or an important project for work.

This type of assessment is known as a performance-based assessment. There are a variety of assessments that can display what students have learned. Ten of the more common ones are (Stanley, 2014):

- oral presentations,
- debates/speeches,
- role playing,
- group discussions,
- interviews,
- portfolios,
- exhibitions,
- essays,
- research papers, and
- journals/student logs. (p. 43)

These are all effective final assessments that display authentic learning. They also all provide lifelong skills beneficial to students. If you can write a good essay, interview others, or create a portfolio that could potentially be used down the road to show your ability, these are long-term benefits provided by these types of evaluations and authentic learning.

Interactive

Probably the greatest benefit to authentic learning is the interactive nature of it. Many traditional classrooms are not very active. Students sit in rows, working on individual work or idly listening to a lecture while taking notes. The teacher stands in front of the class giving direct instruction, and the students merely sit there and receive it. Basically, students are being given the fish, rather than being taught how to fish. Truly effective authentic learning, however, requires students to get out of their seats and be involved in the learning.

In the interactive classroom, you might see 30 different students working on 30 different products. They might be working in groups; they might be working with a mentor. Students' desks are scattered throughout the classroom, rather than lined up in perfect rows all pointed toward the front. Most important to this interactive classroom, more voices are heard than just the teacher's. In fact, if done correctly, the teacher is not talking much at all. The students are asking the questions of one another, challenging themselves, and guiding the direction the learning is going. The students are not interacting with the teacher; they are interacting with the learning.

In addition to involvement, the interactive nature of authentic learning allows for creativity. Different students have different levels of creativity. The performance-based aspect of authentic learning allows students to tap into their creativity, for example, as they determine how to demonstrate their learning in a final product at the end of a unit. If a student is very creative and skilled at drawing, he or she could choose to exhibit artwork related to the subject of the unit. If his or her creativity comes in the ability to sew, he or she might role-play a character or real-life figure from the unit complete with a costume. If students are provided opportunities to choose ways to display their creativity, the possibilities are endless.

An ancillary effect of interactive learning is that it is not only engaging for students, but it is also engaging for the teacher. If set up correctly, students are the drivers of their learning and are actively learning while the teacher gets to observe and coach along the way. In the end, it is much more exciting than giving students a worksheet and watching them while they work on it.

KEEPING IT AUTHENTIC

For any lesson you create you have a litmus test you can hold it up to in order to ensure it is one of authentic learning. The checklist boils down to four items (Rule, 2006):

1. An activity that involves real-world problems and that mimics the work of professionals; the activity involves presentation of findings to audiences beyond the classroom.
2. Use of open-ended inquiry, thinking skills and metacognition.
3. Students engage in discourse and social learning in a community of learners.
4. Students direct their own learning. (p. 2)

If you are missing any of these elements, your lesson might not be as authentic as you think. Ask yourself: If you added the missing element(s), how much better would the lesson be?

2 Chapter

The Importance of 21st-Century Skills

The illiterate of the 21st century will not be those who cannot read and write, but those who cannot learn, unlearn, and relearn.

—Alvin Toffler

Students need to be prepared for the future. In order to do that, we need to make sure our classrooms are places where 21st-century skills—skills that enable students to function and thrive in the future world that awaits them—are taught. Often, we get bogged down with content. Although content has its value in the classroom, what is its value in the real world? If you are a writer, understanding foreshadowing would be of value, but not if you are a landscape architect. If you are an engineer, the ability to work with fractions would be important, but not to a copy editor. As much as social studies teachers want every child to know the Constitution, it is not a necessary requirement for being a citizen. Students learn a lot of content they will never use again. How does a teacher ensure students will be prepared for the future if their future does not involve using the content being taught? The answer is to center the content on 21st-century skills that will translate into and be useful in any profession. In taking this approach, not only are students learning the content, but they also are gaining skills that will be beneficial to them no matter what they are learning.

Authentic Learning

21ST-CENTURY SKILLS

In a Hanover Research (2011) report, "A Crosswalk of 21st Century Skills," its authors analyzed six major educational frameworks designed to improve the development of 21st-century skills. This report included critical skills listed by the Partnership for 21st Century Skills, Tony Wagner's Seven Survival Skills from the book *The Global Achievement Gap* (2008), the Metiri Group's enGauge framework, the Iowa Core 21st Century Skills developed by the Iowa Department of Education, the Connecticut State Department of Education, and the Assessment and Teaching of 21st Century Skills (ATC21S).

Each of these frameworks is slightly different than the others, but they agree on certain things (Hanover Research, 2011). For example, each framework focuses on four critical areas of development:

■ collaboration and teamwork,

■ creativity and imagination,

■ critical thinking, and

■ problem solving (p. 5).

There is also a second tier of important skills present amongst all of the frameworks, including flexibility and adaptability, global and cultural awareness, information literacy, and leadership. Four other skills also appear in a majority of the frameworks: oral and written communication skills, social responsibility and citizenship, technology literacy, and initiative.

Each of these skills alone cannot create a 21st-century learner, but the combination of them can. In order to understand these skills better, we should define what each skill means, what the skill involves, and why it will be important in your 21st-century classroom. The following sections look more in depth at (1) collaboration, (2) creativity, (3) critical thinking, (4) problem solving, (5) adaptability, (6) global awareness, (7) information literacy, (8) leadership, (9) citizenship/social responsibility, (10) effective oral and written communication, (11) technology literacy, and (12) initiative.

Collaboration

Collaboration needs to be taught to students. No matter what the situation, you are going to be working with others for the rest of your life. Whether you go into business, enter the military, or start a family, you have to learn to work effectively and collaborate to produce the desired outcome. That is why collaboration is such a valuable skill for students to learn. It is often a skill we do not teach in the classroom, however (Stanley, 2016). We might put students together for a group project, pair students up to work out a problem, or ask them to help one another. But how much purposeful, guided collaboration takes place in the classroom?

One way to ensure collaboration practice is to make sure each student understands his or her role in the group and exactly what is expected. This can sometimes be confusing because a student is unsure of what he or she is supposed to be doing or is just waiting around for someone to tell him or her what to do. Instead, when you create your groups, give everyone a specific role, such as recorder, speaker, leader, timekeeper, or task manager. This results in two things: (1) Students know what their task is. There is no sitting around waiting to be told what to do because it has very clearly been defined. (2) Students are held accountable. This negates the unfair feelings many students experience when working in groups—that even though they worked hard, one "bad" group member pulls their grade down by not contributing to the group as much.

Authentic learning often takes the form of group work, so being able to collaborate well is going to make for better outcomes. Because you are working with students on the ability to collaborate, one natural byproduct is that you will be teaching students leadership skills. This results in someone with the confidence to step forward, share ideas, make others feel as though he or she is listening to their ideas, and inspire others to accomplish great things. Collaboration, which is discussed further in Chapter 5, is an invaluable skill to any 21st-century student.

Creativity

The ability to generate ideas leads to the skill of creativity. The more comfortable students get with thinking critically, or outside-of-the-box thinking, the more creative their ideas are going to be. Although certain people are born being more creative than others, creativity is something that can be fostered and taught. Trilling and Fadel (2009) attributed creativity as starting with imagination (p. 57). The question becomes: How do you allow students to use their imaginations in the age of content standards that do not really ask for that skill? If our classrooms focus too heavily on facts, recall, simple skills, and test-taking, students will not be ready to think creatively in the real world. As Sir Kenneth Robinson, a thought leader on creativity, explained (as cited in Trilling & Fadel, 2009):

Authentic Learning

Traditional education's focus . . . has not been good for the development of creativity and innovation. This is changing in the 21st century, and education systems from Finland to Singapore are beginning to put creativity and innovation as a high priority in their desired outcomes for student learning. (p. 57)

We need to generate ways for students to use their creativity and innovation in the classroom, while linking to content standards. The simple solution is more choice. The more choice you give students, the more opportunities there will be to be creative in their demonstration of what they learned. This could be choices in topics, choices in products, and/or choices in the depth of learning.

Providing students with choice allows for much creativity and innovation. Choice is something that, by its nature, authentic learning allows for. Instead of prescribing the product, a teacher can allow students to come up with their own ideas. They have the space to be creative and innovative.

Critical Thinking

Critical thinking is being able to think at a higher level. This spans Levels 3 and 4 on Webb's (2005) depth of knowledge (see Table 1). The first two levels are considered lower depths of knowledge. Can a student recall information he or she has been told? Can he or she understand a concept? We want all students to be able to function at these levels. The challenge for teachers is to tap into those higher depths of knowledge. Can students reason something out, looking at multiple perspectives and solutions? Can they extend that thinking even further, coming up with a completely different answer or result?

Besides thinking at a higher depth of knowledge, the advantage of being able to think critically is that you have multiple ideas for the same problem. Again, how valued would a future employee be who has the ability to do this?

Problem Solving

The ability to problem solve is a skill students will use for the rest of their lives. Think about the worth an employee with strong problem-solving skills would be to an employer. After all, solving problems creatively and effectively saves money and leads to new clients. Although it seems at times like those with the ability to problem solve

TABLE 1

Depth of Knowledge

Depth of Knowledge	
Level 1	Recall of a fact
Level 2	Use information or conceptual knowledge
Level 3	Strategic thinking that requires reasoning and usually more than one answer
Level 4	Extended thinking that requires time to think and process

Note. Adapted from Webb, 2005.

just have an innate ability to do so, somewhere in their experiences they learned this skill.

There are ways to teach this in the classroom. Math is an excellent vehicle for problem solving. Attempting to determine a solution or even deciding which formula to use for a particular problem are methods of problem solving. With math, however, there is often only a single correct answer. In order to develop a creative problem solver, we need to develop problem-solving situations where there are numerous possibilities and where students can think of any number of creative ways to tackle the situation.

An important aspect of problem solving is the time spent reflecting. We often say to students, "A mistake is not a mistake if you learned from it," but this is something that needs to be taught. How does one learn from a mistake? That is part of the problem-solving process. Why did something not work? What could have been done differently to get a better result? What did you see others doing that might have produced more success for you? Students need to be provided a structure and space for purposeful reflection.

Adaptability

Adaptability is one's ability to react to change. This is a valuable skill in the 21st century because we are developing technology at breakneck speed. It does not take more than a year or two to develop the newest technology that makes the old one obsolete. Those who are able to adapt to these changes often find much success. Those who are not able to keep up might find their skill-set diminish. This is why doctors, lawyers, and teachers must continue learning throughout their careers; otherwise the techniques or procedures they use will become outdated.

Authentic Learning

But how does one teach adaptability in the classroom? Trilling and Fadel (2009) suggested three ways of teaching adaptability, all of which can be accomplished through authentic learning:

> The skills involved in flexibility and adaptability can be learned by working on progressively more complex projects that challenge student teams to change course when things aren't working well, adapt to new developments in the project, and incorporate new team members on both current and new projects. (p. 77)

The ability to change course when things are not working well and adapt to new developments comes in the time management of a project. Students must learn to manage their time within the framework of the deadline and adjust accordingly. Being able to adapt to new group members is part of the collaboration effort, one of the characteristics of authentic learning. If a group is functioning well, adding a new member should not be an issue. It is when a group is barely holding itself together that the introduction of someone new can cause it to implode. This is why proper collaboration is also such a valuable skill.

Global Awareness

The world is flat, according to Thomas Friedman's (2005/2007) thought-provoking book. *The World Is Flat* explores how the world is becoming a much smaller place. With the increased technology of smartphones, the Internet, and Amazon's amazing 2-day (or even same-day) delivery, anything is just moments away. This is why it is very important for students to have an awareness of the world around them.

Of course, this can be a challenge at times when you are teaching teenagers who only see 5 feet in front of them. How do you help students become more globally aware? The best way is to expose them to what is going on around the world. Thirty years ago this would have meant reading the newspaper, watching CNN, or taking a trip to another country. Technology has been a major bridge of gaps. You can Skype with someone in China at the touch of a button, talk to someone in India without paying ridiculously high long-distance fees, or e-mail anyone in the world and not have to wait for a month for a reply by mail, as we used to when we had pen pals.

You can also expose students to global perspectives through the use of foreign-born speakers, arranging these speakers through the local college universities, parents or friends of students in the school, ethnic societies, or other contacts you might have.

These speakers can come in or Skype and give a perspective from someone who comes from a different culture. This point of view can help students to understand global awareness and that other people might see things completely different than they do. In addition to talking about their experiences of being from and living in another country, speakers can answer students' questions directly. (This will be discussed in more depth in Chapter 11.)

It is important for students to have this global awareness because, since 1965, the number of foreign-born people living in the United States has quadrupled to 43 million, according to the Center for American Progress (CAP Immigration Team & Nicholson, 2017). In addition, the diversity of foreign-born people has increased. In the 1960s, 75% of immigrants came from Europe, but by 2015, this number dropped to 11%, with most immigrants coming from Mexico, China, and India. The chance that students are going to interact with someone who is not originally from their home country is very likely.

In addition, there are more and more Americans who are going abroad to study or work. The State Department estimated that 6.3 million Americans are studying or working in a foreign country, the highest number ever (as cited in Matchar, 2012). The youth of today are more likely to go overseas than those a generation before, with the percentage of Americans ages 25 to 34 who are planning to move overseas going from less than 1% to 5.1%. Among 18- to 24-year-olds, 40% are interested in moving abroad, up from 12% in 2007. Having a global awareness in which students are accepting of different cultures is going to make this opportunity more likely.

Information Literacy

Trilling and Fadel (2009) defined *information literacy* as the ability to:
- access information efficiently and effectively,
- evaluate information critically and competently, and
- use information accurately and creatively (p. 65).

Like all 21st-century skills, information literacy is a skill for life (Stanley, 2016). Being able to determine where and how to efficiently, effectively, critically, and competently access information is crucial if you are trying to get to a place you have never been before, discern which new smartphone you should buy, or explain to someone how to create his or her own birdhouse. This skill reaches beyond the classroom and into the real world, as valuable workers are able to perform it with competency and confidence. Any time you are having students conduct research in the authentic classroom—through print or electronic resources—information literacy is a skill that should be taught effectively.

Teachers often assume students have already been taught information literacy, especially when working with older students (Stanley, 2016). The problem, however, is that some students have not been shown how to access and analyze information properly. Information literacy is a skill that must be taught purposefully. Introducing or reviewing the basics through a mini-lesson could be helpful to students in any grade. Ensuring students have an understanding of how to properly research, utilizing both print and electronic resources, is not something you should take for granted. For example, if students were required to search the web to find information, it would be beneficial to cover some important skills, such as:

- how to create a search using keywords,
- which search engines are best for certain types of inquiries,
- determining whether a website can be trusted or not, and
- how to paraphrase information and properly cite sources (p. 17).

Leadership

Leadership is one of those skills that is not explicitly taught in the classroom but that everyone agrees is a valuable skill to possess. The problem is: How does one teach someone to be a leader? Some believe that leaders are born—that from birth these individuals have a certain innate ability to be a good leader. Others believe that leadership can be taught, but what does that look like?

Like most things, there is a little bit of truth to both of these beliefs. There are people who seem to exude leadership, even at a very young age, either due to confidence, charisma, or being well-spoken. But leadership can be nurtured as well. Someone who does not possess the aforementioned skills can learn strategies to leading—especially when what leadership looks like is broken down into skills. According to Bill McBean (2012), in his book *The Facts of Business Life: What Every Successful Business Owner Knows That You Don't*, the five qualities of a good leader are:

1. flexibility,
2. communication,
3. patience,
4. humility and presence, and
5. being responsible (pp. 47–48).

Notice that many of these characteristics overlap with the 21st-century skills discussed in this chapter. Thus, if you teach students the other 21st-century skills, they are likely to become good leaders. This usually involves putting them in a situation where they can exhibit these characteristics. Consider collaboration, discussed in much more detail in Chapter 5. By working in groups, students learn the skills of flexibility, communication, patience, humility, and being responsible.

Citizenship/Social Responsibility

Citizenship, like leadership, is one of those intangible qualities that cannot be assessed on a state test, and yet, it is highly valued. Previously, a good citizen was someone who voted, was loyal to his or her country, and obeyed the laws. Citizenship has evolved over the years from being something you *are* to being something you *do*. Being a good citizen still means doing all of those things, but much like the world becoming flat, there is now a bigger picture of taking social responsibility. In schools, citizenship can be taught through service learning. Service learning, as defined by Barbara Jacoby (1996) in her book *Service-Learning in Higher Education*, is:

> a form of experiential education in which students engage in activities that address human and community needs together with structured opportunities for reflection designed to achieve desired learning outcomes. (p. 5)

Service learning is a combination of school learning and life learning. While learning about energy conservation in science class, students could participate in a recycling drive. While reading the book *Hoot* by Carl Hiaasen, the class could find a way to preserve the homes of birds in a neighborhood that is being built. In social studies, students could learn about politics by working on a campaign, explore global issues and organizations that support them while participating in Model United Nations, or experience economics while raising money for a needy family during the holidays.

Citizenship can certainly be taught without service learning, but if you want to make your classroom an authentic one where students are taking social responsibility, there is no better way than having students get involved in the community.

Authentic Learning

✳Effective Oral and Written Communication

Public speaking is a valuable skill because not everyone succeeds at it, but the more opportunities you give your students to gain experience, the more comfortable they will become (Stanley, 2016). Public speaking skills:

1. increase self-confidence,
2. make you more comfortable around other people,
3. are the most effective ways to get your message across,
4. can boost performance in other areas in life,
5. allow you to demonstrate your knowledge,
6. allow you to improve upon your knowledge,
7. differentiate you in the workplace, and
8. can help make you a leader.

When students are out in the real world seeking jobs, there are millions of people trying to do the same thing. What will make someone stand out from the crowd? What will allow potential employers to notice them over others? The ability to publicly speak is one of those skills.

Learning what goes into a successful or effective public presentation is also important to teach. From the use of body language and tone of voice, to the persuasiveness of the speaker and confidence, there are several skills students can work on and get better at. The more public speaking students do in your authentic class, the more confidence students gain and the better they are going to get at it.

Technology Literacy

Technology literacy is the ability to use technology to learn. It is amazing how technology has evolved education over the course of the last 20 years. There are many schools and districts that are now one-to-one, providing a device for every student. Teachers have to keep up with the technology that children began learning at birth. But technology literacy is more than simply putting the device in the hands of students. They have to be shown properly how to use technology literacy to their academic advantage, as well as understand the role of digital citizenship. According to the Alliance for Childhood, there are three main aspects of technology literacy (Cordes, Monke, & Talbot, n.d.):

1. Knowing how to use or operate particular tools.
2. Understanding, at least in a rudimentary way, how they work.

3. Developing the capacity to think critically, for one's self, about the entire realm of designing, using, and adapting technologies to serve personal, social, and ecological goals in ways that will sustain life on Earth. (para. 3)

Finding ways for student to incorporate technology into their learning is authentic in that the chances they end up using technology in their lives and jobs are very high.

Initiative

Authentic learning requires self-direction. Because there is much choice and students are the ones who determine how they are learning, having such a skill is instrumental to success (Stanley, 2016). There are benefits to this strategy, including, as Ryan and Grolnick (1986) noted, "When individuals feel more like origins than pawns, they have higher self-esteem, feel more competent, and perform at higher levels of accomplishment" (p. 550). The teacher should act as a guide. He or she should allow students to direct themselves, occasionally offering resources and guidance. Through this approach, students become self-directed learners. As Stanley (2016) noted:

> How valued would a person be to [his or her] employer if he or she takes initiative and does not need to be watched to make sure he is working? Would not you as the teacher want a classroom full of these students? You would be able to do what is every teacher's dream: teach. (p. 19)

When students are self-directed, students are more motivated and creative because they are not constrained, and they tap into those higher levels of thinking that you want students to explore.

KEEPING IT AUTHENTIC

It is important for students to have a good grasp of 21st-century skills, not just because it will help them in their schooling, but because it will be a humongous advantage for any job they seek. According to the National Association of Colleges and Employers (2015), the skills businesses are seeking are:
- the ability to work in a team,

Authentic Learning

- the ability to make decisions and solve problems,
- the ability to plan, organize and prioritize work,
- the ability to communicate verbally with people inside and outside an organization,
- the ability to obtain and process information,
- the ability to analyze quantitative data,
- technical knowledge related to the job,
- proficiency with computer software programs,
- the ability to create and/or edit written reports, and
- the ability to sell and influence others.

All of these are covered by the 21st-century skills discussed in this chapter. Having these skills teaches students life and career skills that will benefit them in the real world.

3
Chapter

Exploring Rigor and Relevance

Authentic teaching and learning requires a live encounter
with the unexpected. An element of suspense and surprise, an
evocation of that which we did not know until it happened.
If these elements are not present, we may be training or
indoctrinating students, but we are not educating them.

—Parker Palmer

Learning 21st-century skills is something that will not only help students when they get to the next grade, but also will help them in college, in their career, and in life. Students will spend the rest of their lives learning, whether at work, home, church, or play. To heighten the effect of this authenticity, the teacher should try to bring in the real world as much as possible or have students participate in outside experiences as part of the lesson.

DOMAIN D

In the real world, tasks are almost always performance-based assessment. Scientists, mathematicians, engineers, and researchers are not taking a test, but are actually cre-

Authentic Learning

ating new theories, products, and ideas. This is what authentic learning in the classroom allows the teacher to provide for students—the ability to create. More than that, students can perform real-world tasks. This allows you to reach Domain D of the Rigor/Relevance framework developed by the International Center for Leadership in Education (as cited in Jones, 2004). The framework is shown in Figure 3. Domain D is a combination of getting to higher levels of thinking, such as analysis, synthesis, and evaluation, that authentic learning allows for students, while applying that thinking to a real-world situation. Jones (2004) defined Domain D as the following:

> Students have the competence to think in complex ways and also apply knowledge and skills they have acquired. Even when confronted with perplexing unknowns, students are able to use extensive knowledge and skill to create solutions and take action that further develops their skills and knowledge. (p. 4)

Here are some of the examples of lessons Jones (2004) provided for what Domain D looks like:

- Language arts:
  - Simulate a presidential debate.
  - Write a legal brief defending a school policy.
  - Prepare a demonstration video (p. 8).

- Mathematics:
  - Create formulas to predict changes in stock market values.
  - Design support posts of different materials and size to handle stress load in a building.
  - Develop a sampling plan for a public opinion poll (p. 9).

- Science:
  - Explore designs of car safety restraints using eggs in model cars.
  - Design and construct a robot.
  - Discuss the social, ethical, and emotional consequences of genetic testing (p. 10).

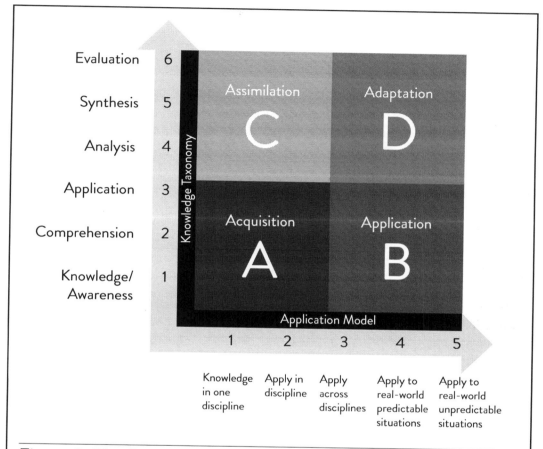

Figure 3. The Rigor/Relevance Framework. From *Rigor/Relevance Framework: A Guide to Focusing Resources to Increase Student Performance* (p. 2), by W. R. Daggett, 2016, Rexford, NY: International Center for Leadership in Education. Retrieved from http://www.leadered.com/pdf/Rigor%20Relevance%20Framework%20White%20Paper%202016.pdf. Copyright 2016 by International Center for Leadership in Education. Reprinted with permission.

- Social studies:
  - □ Analyze a local, state, or national issue and prescribe a response that promotes the public interest or general welfare (e.g., a voter registration campaign).
  - □ Research and debate economic issues and public policy related to the Internet, such as sharing of online music.
  - □ Analyze a school/community problem, suggest a solution, and prepare a plan to solve it (p. 11).

These can all be accomplished with authentic learning.

REAL-WORLD PROBLEMS

According to Stanley (2014), "Using real-world problems involves taking the content you have to teach and connecting it to a real-world situation. . . . It means actually having students produce a product that could be used in the real world or that simulates a real-world situation" (p. 110). For example, if you are teaching persuasive writing, have students write letters to a congressperson about an issue they feel strongly about, rather than an arbitrary essay. Or, rather than reading about rocks in their science textbook, have students collect and study the rocks in their backyards or around the school in order to create a collection that can be analyzed. Instead of learning about immigration through books, have real-life immigrants come into your classroom and share their experiences. Authentic learning requires the teacher to put the lesson in the real world, and real-world problems "enable students to make more of a connection and understand the context of how what they are learning in school fits into everyday life" (p. 110).

There are many benefits to making learning address a real-world problem. For one, a real-world problem connects students to the bigger picture. Many times students have no context for how what they are learning fits into the real world. Having a real-world connection allows students to see the skill being learned applied to something in life, drawing that bridge from theory to practice. Student motivation is also another benefit. By making learning address a real-world problem, you are challenging students to actually solve something that has meaning to it. It is not some problem on a piece of paper that has no implications. By working on a real-world problem, the students create products that are more legitimate because they can actually be used. As

Bruce Alberts, former president of the National Academy of Science, noted (as cited in Curtis, 2001):

> Everybody is motivated by challenge and solving problems, and we don't make use of that in schools enough. Project-based learning gives everybody a chance to sort of mimic what scientists do, and that's exciting. And it's fun if it's done well. (para. 4)

A third benefit is that society itself can benefit from the student work. If you have students conducting a community service project, it makes the city that much better. Or if students are developing a real solution to a real problem, such as determining how to overcome the opioid problem, it could benefit anyone whose life is affected by this issue. Or if middle/high school students develop a plan for a program to mentor elementary students, then those young minds will be influenced by their older peers.

FINAL PRODUCT IN A REAL-WORLD SETTING

How do you make authentic learning real world? There are multiple approaches you can take with this. The first is having students connect to the real world based on their project topics. The second way is to connect through authentic interactions with people, whether they are community members, experts, or mentors. The third strategy is to create a lesson that helps them to reach a future goal. Through these three strategies, here are eight possible kinds of real-world connections (Simpkins, Cole, Tavalin, & Means, 2002):

1. connecting through student interests,
2. connecting through student experiences,
3. connecting through significant issues,
4. improving the real world,
5. relating to clients,
6. interacting with assessors,
7. interacting with people who know, and
8. learning adult work and life skills.

Utilizing student interests is an easy way for students to make real-world connections. Introduce a lesson about something they have chosen and care about. Doing so

Authentic Learning

will improve their level of engagement and motivation, which are strengthened by the choice aspect of authentic learning. For example, in science class, have students choose an experiment to demonstrate the scientific method. Or use math to investigate a sport a student is interested in. Or, in language arts, instead of reading a class book, choose a class theme, and let the students use a book of their choosing as long as it fits within that theme. Any time you can give students choice and have them relate to an interest they have, it is a win-win situation for everyone.

Students have all sorts of experiences they bring with them to school, and connecting them to what is being taught can be very valuable. At the beginning of the year, conduct a poll with students to see if they have any experience with topics you will be studying throughout the year. Then invite them to share these experiences with the class. Students will be hearing firsthand how what they are learning about is used in the real world. You can also expand these experiences to the parents of your students. Send an e-mail to parents early in the year listing the topics that will be covered, and invite parents with experience in a topic to come in and talk to the class. You might get a linguistics expert, who could talk to your class about word origins, or an accountant, who can come in and show how math is used in his everyday job. One of your parents may even be an architect, who could share her experiences with planning and creating an office building or house.

You could connect through significant issues: Find real issues that are affecting the world and bring them to the classroom, including current events such as medical crises, conflicts between countries, financial changes, and newly developed, innovative technology. Work these into the content, using them in English language arts to write editorials and other opinion pieces, debating them in social studies class, or creating a product that shows what students have learned. Because you are giving students the opportunity to connect to the world at large, they will be more passionate and motivated about their learning.

Students want the world to be a better place. They are usually very idealistic and see the good in things much more readily than adults. If you give them a chance to improve the real world through a lesson, they will take the ball and run with it. Setting up your lessons so that students are bringing about change in their school, community, state, or even nation is something that will resonate with them. This allows students to conduct real research, rather than just looking up something someone else has already done. It allows students to create.

Partner with local businesses. If the lesson involves the construction of something, contact an engineering firm. If students are learning about economics, partner with local banks and find out if they already have a program for teaching students. If students are learning about the government or law, is there a law firm that could be a potential partner, or are there city hall employees you could work with? Making these partnerships bridges the gap between school and the business community.

One way to have students participate in a professional learning network is to bring in outside experts to evaluate the final product. Students may be presenting to a panel of businesspeople or giving a lesson to students much older than them. The audience might be the public invited to participate or a group very specific to the topic at hand. Bringing in an outside expert to evaluate:

- gives students another viewpoint in the assessment other than the teacher's,
- makes the project authentic because the audience is professionals rather than just fellow students,
- ramps up the expectations and makes them more rigorous because the audience is made up of experts who have seen what a professional product looks like,
- engages the community and makes them part of the educational process, and
- connects students to the real world by giving them experience in presenting to professionals and learning valuable 21st-century skills in the process.

Through this authentic learning, students can create a body of work to share with colleges or prospective employers to demonstrate how they work and the quality of work they produce. Unlike objective tests and worksheets that eventually get tossed in the trash can, students can create a portfolio of their work that will be useful to them in the future.

CREATING LESSONS WITH YOUR STUDENTS

A great way to both make a lesson authentic and have students see the context of how it fits into the real world is to have the students create the lesson themselves. Use a topic that needs to be covered, and create an essential question, or the learning objective you want students to meet. Then, have students brainstorm or research online possible ideas to build the lesson. This would involve them choosing the product, envisioning the timeline, and developing the learning objectives and skills they need to meet. You could even make it a competition by dividing students into groups to see which group produces the best idea. There would be certain parameters and constraints the proposal would have to include. Proposed lessons would:

- first and foremost, enable those involved to learn;
- need to have a final product;

Authentic Learning

- allow participants, in addition to learning the content, to learn a 21st-century skill (i.e., public speaking, creating a portfolio, formation of a business plan, etc.);
- not be any shorter than 2 weeks and not take any longer than 4 weeks from start to finish;
- need to mention what resources will be needed for students;
- include an idea of how progress will be assessed/evaluated;
- employ higher level thinking skills; and
- ideally, tie into modern times or have a practical application.

Provide students with a structure and further instruction for presenting their proposals. For example, the proposal:

- needs to be an oral presentation,
- should take no more than 5 minutes to explain,
- can use visuals, and
- can include a syllabus.

Students should be prepared to answer follow-up questions at the end of their presentations. Once the proposals have been presented and one has been chosen, you could connect the lesson even further to students by creating the rubric to evaluate the product together. Students are going to be much more motivated when working on a project of their own devising.

KEEPING IT AUTHENTIC

According to Rule (2006), the basic formula for authentic learning is the sum of four aspects:

- real-world problems,
- higher level thinking,
- a community of learners, and
- student-directed learning. (p. 1)

A real-world problem combines with the other three aspects, which naturally come with learning, to make it authentic. This will take students to Domain D of the Rigor/Relevance Framework (Jones, 2004) and allow for a higher quality of learning in your classroom.

4 Chapter

Inquiry-Based Learning

The art of teaching is the art of assisting discovery.
—Mark Van Doren

Inquiry-based learning is where authentic learning starts because inquiry is learning at its most authentic. Think about when you were a child. When you wanted to learn something as a toddler, you did not wait for someone to fashion a lesson plan or establish a curriculum for you to follow. No, most likely you were curious about something, which caused you to want to learn how to do it. This could be anything from how to walk, how to speak, or how to turn a doorknob. You may have had to learn some tough lessons—the fireplace glass is hot, cats do not like when you pull their tails, and your dad really gets mad when you use rocks to write on his car—but it is through this inquiry that you learned.

Inquiry carries you into your first years of schooling. Everything seems so new and shiny, and you are literally like a sponge, soaking it all in. Because there is so much you do not know, you are curious about so much. Through inquiry, you learn a lot of the building blocks you will use for the rest of your life, such as spelling, basic math, citizenship, and the fact that the world is round. Inquiry is not only used at school. Think about the kid who explores the creek in his backyard, the girl who watches YouTube videos and reproduces intricate arts and crafts from them, or the child who decides to create his own language. Because of this initial curiosity, elementary school classrooms

Authentic Learning

are full of enthusiasm and children who love to learn. They are also full of teachers who are trying to capture this enthusiasm and translate it to learning the fundamentals. Elementary teachers facilitate lots of hands-on learning, whether it be coloring, cutting and pasting, playing duck-duck-goose, or using manipulatives to learn how to count. You could walk into almost any second-grade classroom in the country, and you will not find students facing the front of the room while the teacher lectures at them. Elementary classrooms are noisy and full of action and have wonderful energy.

But as you begin to advance in the school system, inquiry and curiosity begin to wane. This is caused by a combination of two factors. One, children know a lot more, so everything is not so new to them. Because of this, the learning is not as exciting as it once was. Secondly, in order to prevent classrooms from being so full of action and noise, junior high and high school teachers resort to a lot of teacher-directed learning. They put students in rows and conduct lectures. Students often do not experience inquiry by asking questions or trying and failing. They are *told* things they are expected to know and will help them later in life. Teachers use the excuse of trying to prepare students for college, where they will be lectured at for hours at a time, but this is just an excuse. Older children and teens still possess a love of learning. They still have that inquiry inside of them. They just use it for their own pursuits, such as driving, dating, partying, and sports.

What if we could make all students curious about school again? What if we could fan the embers of inquiry and get it blazing again? The good news is we can. The key is bringing inquiry back into the classroom—no matter the grade level.

WHAT IS INQUIRY-BASED LEARNING?

Inquiry-based learning is a teaching strategy where, instead of the teacher presenting facts, there is a question, problem, or scenario posed for students to consider. Students then identify and research items in order to come up with a solution, organically expanding their knowledge in the process. What they learn is what they have discovered, not what the teacher has given them. The learning is student-centered and active, meaning students will be engaged. The teacher takes on the role of a facilitator who guides the students, often with questions that will expand the thought process, rather than answers that will stifle it.

This teaching style might seem overwhelming or frightening to a teacher in today's classroom where the Common Core State Standards or other national or state standards need to be taught prior to annual student testing that holds the teacher accountable for what his or her students learn. With standards and goals to meet, it does not feel like we have time to let students wander around, pursuing dead ends. There are more traditional teachers who would argue we have to streamline the classroom so we are covering all of the standards we need to. In actuality, inquiry-based learning reinforces curriculum content. More than that, inquiry-based lessons are enduring. Because inquiry-based lessons are built upon the curiosity of students, this sparks their brains to better remember what they have learned. If a student memorizes a content standard just long enough to take the test, he or she is not going to be able to recall it later. Why waste your time teaching students something they are just going to forget? Would you not want to make sure the time you are spending in the classroom is efficient and getting the biggest bang for its buck?

In addition to reinforcing curriculum content, inquiry-based learning has many other advantages. Some of these include (Guido, 2017):

- **Deeper understanding of content:** Because students develop the questions they explore, they are of course going to have a better understanding of a lesson. They take ownership of their learning because they came up with how to study the content.

- **Making learning rewarding:** The reward for doing well in a class is usually a good grade. What if it were more than that? Because students are part of the learning process, the learning becomes the reward, not the approval of the teacher.

- **Building initiative and self-direction:** Students guide what is being learned. They do not need to wait for the teacher to tell them how to proceed. This causes students to draw their own conclusions and, essentially, teaches students how to learn on their own.

- **Differentiated instruction:** Because students are choosing what to learn, they also choose how to learn it and at what level. Inquiry-based learning allows students to learn at the level they are capable of. If you have three students researching whether renewable energy sources are effective, one of them might find a simple article that gives the basics, another might use a more complex article that goes into deeper detail, while a third might find an academic thesis and use that information.

- **No ceiling:** If you ask a student a question with only one correct answer, once the student gets that answer, the learning is done. Inquiry-based learning tends to have more open-ended questioning. This means the sky is the limit, and students can endlessly explore a topic. Because they can explore it in great depth, there is little chance of them reaching an end too quickly.

WHY USE INQUIRY-BASED LEARNING?

In addition to the benefits to students, there are advantages of inquiry-based learning to teachers, which include (MacKenzie, 2017):

- increasing motivation and engagement,
- promoting enduring understanding, and
- giving students ownership of their learning.

When students are engaged, a more pleasant classroom results, and students actually learn. Inquiry-based learning makes the classroom a partnership rather than a dictatorship. For the teacher, this takes the brunt of the responsibility of learning off his or her shoulders and puts it on the ones who should be working the hardest—the students. Inquiry-based learning (MacKenzie, 2017):

- nurtures student passion and talents,
- empowers student voice and honors student choice,
- fosters student curiosity and a love of learning, and
- invites students to solve real-world problems.

What could be better for students than a classroom that is engaging and promotes interest in what they are learning about? A classroom where you go to school and actually learn? More than that, a classroom where students learn how to learn because students no longer need the teacher to create a lesson plan or feed them information? Students have the ability to do that for themselves. As well as this skill, there are additional 21st-century survival skills that students could develop through inquiry-based learning. Some of these are (MacKenzie, 2017):

- grit, perseverance, and self-direction;
- strong research skills; and
- the ability to ask questions in seeking to understand.

How authentic are these skills? How much success not just in school, but in life, would students have if they were equipped with them?

The importance of grit cannot be undersold. In her seminal book, *Grit*, Angela Duckworth (2016) proposed a theory about the development of *grit*, which is a combination of a person's perseverance and passion: She theorized it is among the most important predictors of success. Inquiry-based learning teaches this skill because it is driven by the motivation and persistence of the student, not the teacher. When something gets tough, students have to learn to push through on their own, not because the teacher told them to. This develops grit.

Students will certainly develop strong research skills, as they are the ones who will be finding the resources that drive their inquiry. Through this process, they will learn what works, what does not, what websites are reliable, which ones to avoid, and what is the best way to conduct a search. And then when the lesson is over, students will still possess these skills, which they can use the next time they need to find something, even if it is not related to their academics.

The entire purpose of inquiry-based learning is that the students ask the questions that drive the learning. The more students do this, the better they will get at asking the thought-provoking, rich questions that allow for a lot of inquiry. This skill will translate to real life, where they will become very adept at asking these types of questions in their relationships, in their work life, and in their own personal beliefs.

From all of these advantages, the logical question should not be, "Why should I use inquiry-based learning?" But rather, "Why would I not want to use inquiry-based learning?"

WHAT DOES INQUIRY-BASED LEARNING LOOK LIKE IN THE CLASSROOM?

If you walked into a classroom that was using inquiry-based learning, what would it look like? One thing is for sure: It would look very different than your traditional classroom. Instead of the teacher leading the discussion or driving the lesson, the students are in the driver's seat.

Inquiry-based learning follows a particular cycle (see Figure 4).

You can see this cycle demonstrated in the following example, which shows what an inquiry-based lesson might look like in a science class. Students ask essential questions and then research them in order to find answers. They create their conclusions based on this research and share and discuss their findings with fellow classmates. Finally, they reflect on what was learned from going through this process:

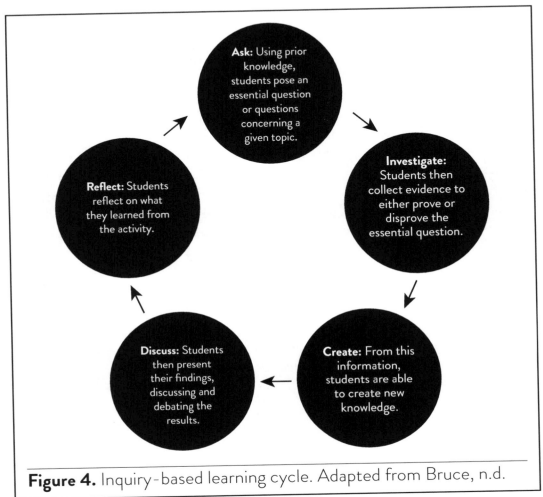

Figure 4. Inquiry-based learning cycle. Adapted from Bruce, n.d.

A teacher introduces a lesson on the layers of the Earth. In order to generate ideas, the teacher goes to the board and writes the term, "layers of the Earth." Then, she asks the class, "What do you know about the layers of the Earth that you find interesting, or what would you like to learn more about?" Students begin to generate ideas, shouting them out so fast the teacher can barely keep up writing them. "Magma," "crust," "core." Sharing these terms sparks other ones from students, such as specific sections of the layers and their effects on the planet.

The students create a web (see Figure 5) of their responses, with either the teacher adding them or students adding them themselves. Most importantly, the students drive the conversation with no idea being out of bounds. For example, students might get into some nonacademic terms, such as those in Figure 6. It is all right for them to

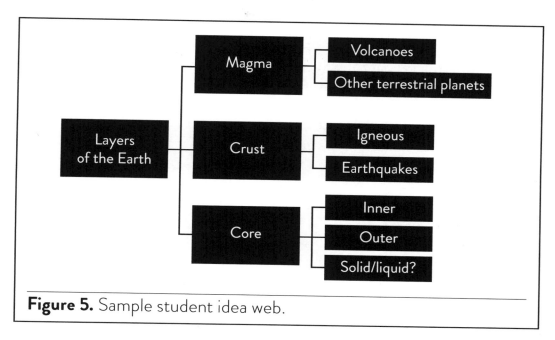

Figure 5. Sample student idea web.

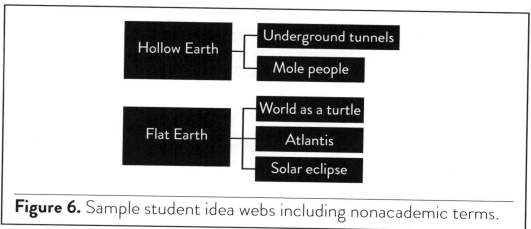

Figure 6. Sample student idea webs including nonacademic terms.

Authentic Learning

explore these topics. The teacher should not be vetoing ideas, but rather encouraging any sort of thinking.

Students then choose a topic that they would like to learn more about. It can be the one they suggested, or it could be one that someone else recommended that they find even more interesting. From these terms, essential questions are created. These essential questions should be open-ended and something that can be supported by research. If a student chooses *inner core* as her term, she could develop a few essential questions, such as:

1. What is the core composed of and at what ratio?
2. How does this core allow the planet Earth to form? What happens without this inner core?
3. What are cores on other planets made of, and how do they affect the makeup of the planets?

From these questions, students begin to create answers through their research. They draw conclusions and make statements based on what they find. Students should then present what they have learned. This could take various forms, such as a lesson for the class, a podcast, a display that shows the answers to their questions, or even a research paper. Students have become experts on their particular topic, so everyone will learn from everyone else, rather than just learning from the teacher. Students' findings are discussed and debated as they are presented, and students gain further insights.

Finally, students close the lesson by reflecting upon what they learned. This could be about content, process, skills, self-awareness, or anything else they got out of the lesson. A reflection can be shared with fellow classmates, it could be conferenced with the teacher, or it could just be something they write in a journal and keep for themselves. This aspect of learning is often overlooked, which is frustrating because this is where the most learning takes place. A student is not telling you what you want to hear; they are sharing what they actually learned. What could be more authentic than that? Reflecting on what they did well, what they could have done better, and what they learned about their own work habits will allow students to become better learners. They will learn from their own experiences, which sounds an awful lot like authentic learning.

TYPES OF INQUIRY-BASED LEARNING

There are various ways to use inquiry in the classroom, running the spectrum of teacher control to complete student control. Where your classroom lies is determined by how much control you are willing to give up. That is one of the more difficult aspects of authentic learning and using inquiry-based learning or one of the other teaching strategies shared in this book: The prospect of not being in complete control of the classroom can be quite uncomfortable for some. Teachers are often made to feel as though they have to be the ones running the show. The major problem with constant teacher-led learning is that it makes students passive participants in their education. If you partake in teacher-directed learning, students will never know how to learn for themselves. Once they are out of school and you take the teacher away, students have difficulty because they no longer have anyone telling them what they should be doing. The students have not authentically learned.

The four types of inquiry are (see Figure 7; Banchi & Bell, 2008):

- **Confirmation Inquiry:** Students follow the lead of the teacher, and everyone follows along at the same pace and same topic as one big class. The teacher is mostly responsible for where the inquiry goes, but the results are likely known in advance.
- **Structured Inquiry:** Students may work individually to answer the questions rather than as a whole group, but the teacher is still the one choosing the topics and identifying the resources students will use.
- **Guided Inquiry:** The teacher chooses the topics, but it is up to the students to decide what the product is going to be.
- **Open Inquiry:** Here the teacher's role is greatly diminished, and it is mostly up to the students to choose their topics, the resources they will use to answer the questions, and what the outcome is going to be.

In a science classroom, these forms of inquiry might look like this:

- **Level 1: Confirmation Inquiry.** In review of a science theme or topic, the teacher would develop questions and a procedure for students to follow, leading to results that are already known. This method is effective in reinforcing concepts and teaching students the rudimentary skills of following procedures, collecting and recording data, and to get a deeper level of understanding.
- **Level 2: Structured Inquiry.** Just like confirmation, the teacher would be the one to provide the initial question as well as the general idea of the procedure

Most teacher control			Least teacher control
Confirmation inquiry	Structured inquiry	Guided inquiry	Open Inquiry

Figure 7. Types of inquiry and the teacher's role. Adapted from Banchi & Bell, 2008.

to follow. Then the students take over control and find ways to explain their results by looking at the research they find.

- **Level 3: Guided Inquiry.** The teacher's only role in this level is to provide the research question. The students would be the ones who create the procedure they are going to use in order to see if that question is accurate or not. They would also come up with the final product where they share what they discovered.
- **Level 4: Open/True Inquiry.** The teacher is completely off the hook in this level, with the students doing everything, including creating the research question, deciding what procedure they will follow, and figuring out how to convey what they have learned to others. It is this level of inquiry you would see at a science fair, where students research something of their own choosing.

When a teacher is just starting out in authentic learning, it might be best to start with the early levels of inquiry-based learning in order to get a feel for it, as well as for the students to get used to it. If you just throw students into inquiry, especially older students who are used to being led by the teacher, this freedom to think and learn might be a bit overwhelming, and the results might be scattered. As the teacher gets more and more comfortable with the inquiry process and the students become familiar with the expectations, then you can begin to move into the deeper levels where students are given more and more leeway to guide their learning.

SETTING THE STAGE

Inquiry-based learning not only changes the role of the teacher, but also alters the role of the student. The brunt of the learning is no longer on the teacher. The students are responsible for deciding the course their learning is going to take. The teacher's main role is to fan the flames of curiosity. This is easier said than done. How does a teacher help students adjust to this shift in learning and maintain a level of inquisitiveness?

First, the teacher needs to promote the spirit of inquiry in the classroom. Students need to be comfortable with the fact that they can explore their curiosities without fear of being reprimanded or told they are wrong. Part of this is making sure that students feel that they can ask any question. As teachers, we often tell students there are no stupid questions, but do we model this behavior in the classroom? When a student asks a teacher a question that seems to be off topic, the teacher typically reacts in one of two ways: She either tries to get the student back to her line of questioning, or she praises the student for trying but moves onto something else. Neither one is very productive. Instead, the teacher would be better served to explore this line of questioning further by asking probing questions. It might look something like this:

> **Teacher:** *(to the class)* What do you think about the idea of isolation in the book *The Adventures of Huckleberry Finn*?
>
> **Kara:** Why do you suppose he named the character Huck Finn?
>
> **Teacher:** That's an excellent question. What do you think?
>
> **Kara:** I dunno. Maybe he just liked the way it sounded. I always have to be careful when saying it quickly because it almost comes out as a bad word.
>
> **Teacher:** One easy way to remedy that is to remember that the character's full name is Huckleberry Finn. Less tempting to curse when using it that way. Does anyone else in the class have any ideas about the naming of the main character?

In this scenario, the teacher has created a classroom environment that promotes the spirit of inquiry. Students like Kara feel comfortable following their curiosities. But the teacher also needs to figure out a way for all students to be involved, not just the compliant ones who raise their hands. Children who need time to process or are more timid may benefit from an alternative way to communicate (Scharaldi, 2016). Some of these methods might include:

- **Use of technology:** We can sometimes be a traditional lot, requiring students to still use pencil and paper to express what they know when there are so many more interesting alternatives, such as PowerPoints, podcasts, FlipGrid, etc.
- **Writing out thoughts in a journal:** Rather than asking a scattershot set of questions and getting immediate answers, allow students to compose their

thoughts in a forum where they can ponder and reflect. They could even record them in Google Forms or an online journal.

- **Conferencing with the teacher:** Manage your classroom so that you can have one-on-one conversations with students while the others are working. You will probably learn a lot about the students from such dialogue.
- **Sharing ideas with a partner or other classmates:** Sometimes students do not want to share with the teacher but would be willing to talk with a peer. Developing reflection protocols to allow them to do this would provide this avenue of bouncing ideas and thoughts off of one another.
- **Longer wait time:** When you ask the class a question, rather than calling on the first hand that goes up, ask instead for students to think about it for a minute or two, or even journal about it, and then ask for responses.

This way all voices are heard. Sometimes it is the quiet ones who have the best ideas, but they are not always given a chance to share.

KEEPING IT AUTHENTIC

Inquiry-based learning is the starting point for authentic learning. If you can master inquiry-based learning, using project-based, problem-based, and/or case-based learning becomes a piece of cake. Inquiry-based learning might seem like a cutting-edge, new educational strategy, but the idea has been around for a long time. John Dewey (1938), one of the framers of 20th-century education, said this:

> There is continuity in inquiry. The conclusions reached in one inquiry become means, material and procedural, of carrying on further inquiries. In the latter, the results of earlier inquiries are taken and used without being resubjected to examination. . . . This immediate use of objects known in consequence of previous mediation is readily confused with immediate knowledge. (p. 140)

It's surprising that this idea, which is nearly 100 years old, actually fits so well with 21st-century education and authentic learning.

5 Chapter

Collaborative Learning

> Collaboration is important not just because it's a better way to
> learn. The spirit of collaboration is penetrating every institution
> and all of our lives. So learning to collaborate is part of equipping
> yourself for effectiveness, problem solving, innovation and
> life-long learning in an ever-changing networked economy.
>
> —Don Tapscott

Collaborative learning is an educational strategy that involves groups of students working together in order to achieve a shared goal. It is a fancy word for group work, but not the group work you did in school, where only one person really worked and the others came along for the ride. True collaborative learning means everyone is doing his or her part, and because they are working together, students can create something they would not have been able to on their own.

Why are collaborative learning skills something 21st-century learners should possess? Because they increase students' value. If someone is able to collaborate with others well and others want to work with him or her, he or she will go far in the real world. Not only can the ability to collaborate help someone in the business world, but it also influences his or her day-to-day activities, whether being with family, playing sports, or interacting with friends. Collaboration is especially valued in the working community because of the importance of *synergy*—the interaction or cooperation of two or more people to produce a combined effect greater than the sum of their separate effects. Thomas Edison created some of the greatest inventions of the 20th century, from the phonograph and motion picture camera, to the fluoroscope and the long-lasting light bulb. He did not invent these alone, however. He assembled a team of investigators who carried out his ideas as well as provided research and development. Edison kept all sorts of different materials and encouraged his team to think outside of the box and try new things. As a team, they were able to create so much more than Edison would have been able to achieve on his own. Do you think Bill Gates or Steve Jobs could have created what they have on their own? It took the combined efforts of many people to produce the breakthroughs of this century.

According to Jones (2010), collaboration can benefit the workplace because it:

- combines different perspectives so that all angles are considered,
- encourages creativity,
- takes advantage of synergies,
- brings balance to decision making, and
- may improve delivery times.

Collaboration means more than just putting students together in a group and hoping they produce a competent product. Teamwork is something that needs to be taught. As the teacher, you need to guide students and foster purposeful collaboration.

TEACHING PURPOSEFUL COLLABORATION

If you value the skill of collaboration in your classroom, you should dedicate some time at the beginning of the school year to teach purposeful collaboration. Purposeful collaboration means that every student is aware of (1) what his or her role in the group is, and (2) what the goal of the group is.

In order to establish a student's role in a group, the group first needs to understand the strengths each person brings to the group. If the group members understand their strengths, as well as their weaknesses, they will know how to best utilize each person. One mistake groups often make is assuming that everyone should work equally as opposed to fairly. Equal work means that everyone works the same amount of time, producing the same amount of work, and giving the same amount of effort. This causes problems because when one group member is doing a task differently than another, it can cause rifts within the group. It is important for members of the group to recognize the differences members of the group have and then assign tasks accordingly. Not only that, it is important to embrace these differences and make sure to take a strengths-based approach to deciding roles for the group.

There are several activities a teacher can facilitate in order for students to learn the strengths of one another. One way is through self- and peer evaluation. Provide students with a stack of sticky notes. Have students use three of their sticky notes to write down what they believe are the three biggest strengths they bring to a team. You might want to demonstrate by doing this yourself, so that students know what sorts of strengths you are looking for. You might even have a prepopulated list of strengths from which they can draw from, such as:

- organized,
- responsible,
- helpful to others,
- stays on task,
- gets along with others,
- follows the rules,
- good public speaker,
- uses time wisely,
- pays attention to detail,
- motivated,
- likes to ask questions,
- good at problem solving,
- gets work done on time,
- does a quality job,
- works with others well,
- thinks about the problem,
- is positive,
- treats others fairly,
- takes initiative, or
- good at discussion.

Either from this list or of their own creation, students list their three strengths (see Figure 8 for an example). Then they take a single sticky note and list their biggest weakness as a group member (see Figure 9). Finally, have students either choose five other students to write a single strength about, or have students divided into groups already and have them evaluate each of their groupmates. It is important to have peers also determine their strengths because sometimes students see themselves one way, but

Figure 8. Student strengths sample activity.

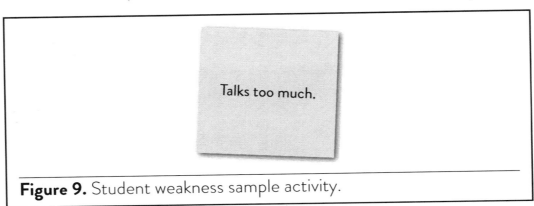

Figure 9. Student weakness sample activity.

other students might see them differently. Getting this outside perspective might give a well-rounded view of a student's true strengths.

From this activity, students will see that their group members bring very different strengths to the whole. Recognizing that they have students in their group who might approach a project differently than they would is important for group harmony and understanding the motivation of others. Group harmony is very different than everyone in the group liking one another. Group harmony is working effectively, despite the fact that group members might not get along, for the benefit and advancement of the project. It is important for the group members to know the group's strengths so that the proper person can carry out certain aspects of the work. For example, if you discover that someone is excellent with technology, put him or her in charge of running the program that creates the presentation. If someone's strength is that he or she is a good public speaker, put him or her in charge of presenting. Why have four people speak, three of whom are clearly not as engaging as the other, when that one person can communicate for the group?

Once students are aware of their strengths, the next step should be a group activity to test their strengths. One such icebreaker activity is the Marshmallow Tower (see Figure 10). An icebreaker activity such as this establishes the foundation for collaborative learning. Once students figure out how members can successfully work together, the next step is to build the endurance for working in a group for a longer-term project. Students might be able to put their differences aside and work together if it is just for one class period, but if they have a 3-week assignment together, can they collaborate to produce a quality product?

SETTING NORMS

One way to establish endurance for longer projects is the use of norms. Norms are very different than rules. Rules are usually determined by an authority figure who is then responsible for enforcing these rules. Norms are simply *expectations*. Do you pick your nose in front of others? There is no rule or law that says you should not do so, but societal norms dictate that doing so is gross or against the normal way of behaving—and you are not judged by one person, but by everyone who has accepted that act as disgusting. Group norms follow the same concept. They are not rules, but they lay out how everyone expects the group members to act when working together. If someone does not follow the group norms, rather than the teacher having to enforce her rules, the students point out how the member is breaking the norm. If you let students create them, norms carry more weight and power. If they are simply rules handed down by the teacher, there is no ownership for students. The fact that students helped to construct their group's norms helps group members remember them better and makes them more instinctual to follow because of this familiarity.

How do you help your class set its norms? Provide students with five to seven sticky notes and the following prompt: "What do you need in order to be successful in a group?" Make sure to frame this in a positive aspect (in other words, do not have students write what causes them to be unsuccessful). Have students draw on their past experiences working in groups and what allowed them to collaborate effectively. Students might need a little guidance in what a successful group looks like. A successful group is one where the members of the group are able to accomplish their task and produce high-quality work. This does not mean members of the group all like one another.

Authentic Learning

Marshmallow Tower

The objective of this is activity is to see which group can build the tallest free-standing structure out of spaghetti, string, and marshmallows.

Materials:

- 20 pieces of uncooked spaghetti noodles per team (not thin)
- 1 yard of kite string per team
- 20 small marshmallows per team

Instructions:

- Introduce two rules: Teams have 20 minutes to build the tallest freestanding structure using only the items provided. *Freestanding* is defined as the structure being able to stand on its own without anyone having to hold it.
- Set a timer for 18 minutes and begin.
- Measure towers at the end.
- Declare a winner!
- Debrief.

Note. This activity provides a short period of time to demonstrate collaboration as a group, but it will reveal whether a person's strengths are indeed what the person says they are. Success in the activity is not about how tall a group can make its tower. Success comes in learning about one another and about oneself. That is why it is important to make sure to take plenty of time to debrief once the challenge is over. More attention should be paid to this debriefing than the construction of students' towers.

Suggested debriefing questions include:
- What did you notice about each person's role in the activity?
- Who seemed to be taking charge? Was this leadership effective?
- Could you see any strengths at work? Give examples.
- Are there any strengths that members of the group said they had but did not display when they could have?

Figure 10. Sample collaboration-building activity.

> - Are there any strengths that members of the group displayed that they did not list as one of theirs?
> - Once group members have established what their strengths are, you can assign specific tasks to members that buoy these strengths. By having specific roles, group members know what their contribution to the group needs to be and can be held accountable if they are not doing their part.
>
> **Figure 10.** Continued.

One thing students and teachers often get confused about is believing members of a group need to get along. They might even create a norm to encourage it, for example, "Be nice to one another." The reality is that not all people get along. For whatever reason, whether past history, attitudes, or a perception, some members of the group are not going to get along with one another, but that is okay. The question students and teachers need to think about is: Is it more important to have someone nice in your group who produces substandard work, or someone who is not as likeable but does a really good job? Businesses would want the second guy. Businesses are not in business so that people can all get along. Businesses are in business to be productive.

Have students write one need per sticky note. After giving them some time to do this, invite them up to the whiteboard or a wall and have them cluster their sticky notes with other students' similar norms. If eight people had something about being respectful, stick all of those sticky notes together. Maybe half of the class thought it was important to meet deadlines. In that case, meeting deadlines becomes a norm. You will quickly see, quite authentically, what is important to the class as a whole. If there is an outlier sticky note with no other similar needs, then the issue is specific to that student and may not be a group norm. From these clusters, create anywhere from five to seven norms the class can agree on (more than seven can cause things to become confusing). It might look something like this:

- Respect others' thoughts, actions, and ideas.
- Everyone needs to contribute to his or her group by doing the task assigned.
- Be willing to share ideas and compromise.
- Stay on task and be willing to refocus when asked.
- Be responsible for the tasks you are assigned.
- Work should be of high quality.

Some norms might need adjustment to fit the needs of all students. For example, if "Get an A on projects" was proposed as a norm, and there were students who are unwilling or unable to meet that norm, then it should not be made a norm. Notice also how all of the norms are put in a positive connotation. They very easily could have looked like this:

- Do not be disrespectful to others' thoughts, actions, and ideas.
- If someone is not contributing, they should be punished.
- Do not block other people's ideas.
- Do not get off task.
- Get done what you say you will get done.
- Work should not be of poor quality.

These norms are similar in spirit, but in looking at both, you can see how the first list will encourage positive collaboration.

Once the list of norms has been formed and all students agree to it, the list should be written or printed, and then displayed in the classroom. You can even provide copies to students and have them keep a copy in their folders. By doing so, students can be constantly reminded of what the norms are, which will help them in their group behavior. Let students know that the norms are not set in stone and can be changed if things do not seem to be working. Maybe an additional norm needs to be included to stop a certain behavior, or one norm does not seem to be effective, so it is stricken from the list. Most importantly, make sure the norms are revisited from time to time to ensure they are not forgotten. Even just going over them again at the beginning of the lesson reminds students of the expectations they created.

DIVIDING UP TASKS

When students are working in groups, it is important to create specific assignments for students. If no specific roles are assigned, everyone in the group will work on everything, which can cause confusion for group members as to exactly what their roles are. This also causes students who are not the most motivated to wait for someone to tell them what to do. If they have a specific role assigned to them, then it is no mystery as to what they should be doing. The various roles should be thought out and planned during the setup of the project. They can be changed as the project goes along to best fit the needs of the group, but starting without established roles makes it difficult for students to know how to start.

Having roles clearly laid out also allows students to hold themselves more accountable. If a particular task is not done, the student responsible can be held responsible, instead of an entire group being blamed. This also eliminates the aspect of small-group work that many students dread—that their grade is dependent upon someone else. Many students are not comfortable with this concept, and rightfully so. Students who have done their work at a high quality should not have their grade affected because someone else decided not to pull his or her weight. Not only that, if you dock other students for work someone else was responsible for, you are not truly assessing the skills of the individual student. A grade should be reflective of the level of skills that student has achieved. The grade should not reflect the inability of someone else to get his or her work done. That should be reflected only in that person's grade.

KEEPING IT AUTHENTIC

Working together is a valuable skill for students to learn. According to Oakley, Felder, Brent, and Elhajj (2004):

> Compared to students taught traditionally, students taught in a manner that incorporates small-group learning achieve higher grades, learn at a deeper level, retain information longer, are less likely to drop out of school, acquire greater communication and teamwork skills, and gain a better understanding of the environment in which they will be working as professionals. (p. 9)

In order to have success in a small-group setting, the teacher must be very purposeful about teaching students how to learn collaboratively. This can be accomplished by making sure students are aware of different strengths each member possesses, creating norms for how students are expected to work in groups, and making sure that roles are clear to students so they are aware of what they should be doing at all times.

6 Chapter

Project-Based Learning

> Seriously, who really cares how long the Nile River is, or who was
> the first to discover cheese? How is memorizing that ever going
> to help anyone? Instead, we need to give kids projects that allow
> them to exercise their minds and discover things for themselves.
>
> —Aaron Swartz

Project-based learning (PBL) is a strategy of teaching that provides many advantages, including (Stanley, 2011):

- allowing for more creativity,
- differentiation of varying ability levels,
- creating a passion for learning, and
- providing authentic opportunities for learning (p. vii).

It is this last advantage that we will focus on in this chapter.

Authentic Learning

WHAT IS PROJECT-BASED LEARNING?

In project-based learning, students are given a task to accomplish. This task usually addresses an essential question, one that reflects an authentic product. It does not need to be as far-reaching as a problem the world is facing, such as global warming or lack of water in Africa, although it certainly could be. Students are either prescribed a product to demonstrate mastery of a concept or are allowed to choose one they feel will demonstrate it. The more choice students are provided, the more creativity they are allowed. PBL is typically long-term, spanning weeks rather than just a single day.

The great thing about PBL is that the teacher can tailor it to meet the needs of the students. The teacher will make decisions regarding the project based on several factors (Stanley, 2011):

- teacher-led versus student-led,
- students working alone versus working in groups,
- curriculum-based versus inquiry-based,
- projects sporadically versus projects consistently, and
- one subject area versus all subject areas (p. 37).

Imagine each of these factors on a spectrum. On each of end of the spectrum is one of the factor's descriptors. Within this spectrum are varying degrees of the descriptors. For example, let us take the first factor and put it on a spectrum (see Figure 11). Even between the ends and the middle are different levels of involvement or lack thereof. Typically, the further to the right of the spectrum you go, the closer you are to authentic project-based learning.

HOW IS PROJECT-BASED LEARNING AUTHENTIC?

How does PBL provide authentic learning opportunities? If the project is designed around a real-world problem or situation, it instantly creates an authentic experience where the solution is something that could actually be used. Consider a nonfiction book, such as *Bulu: African Wonder Dog* by Dick Houston. It is the true story of Anna and Steve Tolan, expatriates from England, who moved to Zambia, Africa. There, they adopted a dog, the runt of a litter, naming him Bulu. The story tells of Bulu's many encounters with African wildlife. Through these various encounters, some dangerous,

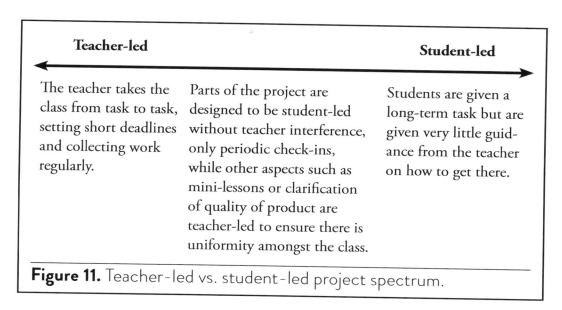

Figure 11. Teacher-led vs. student-led project spectrum.

others heartfelt, the reader is introduced to the plight of the elephant in Africa. Basing a project around a book such as this can create a crosscurricular learning opportunity, connecting language arts (nonfiction informational text) and science (ecosystems), as well as social studies (geography).

In order to make it authentic for students, however, the project needs to be connected to the real world. Using *Bulu*, this can be accomplished by focusing on the Tolans' wildlife conservation efforts: The couple created a conservation education center to teach people how to preserve their environment. Of course, you cannot have students rescuing elephants in their neighborhood, but by focusing on community service through education, and linking it to the book, students can participate in something that is indeed authentic. A project related to the book might look something like Figure 12.

To increase its authenticity, when introducing the project, teachers might consider inviting local nonprofit organizations to visit the classroom and discuss with students what they do and how they educate the public. If you had someone from Amnesty International come in and talk about the treatment of people across the world and how mistreatment can be combatted through education, it would present a real-world problem students might not have been aware of. If you are feeling ambitious, you could have several groups come in and have a presenters' fair. During this event, students can visit various stations, where a representative of the organization explains what the organization does. Students can learn about efforts to educate others about the problem.

Authentic Learning

Community Education Project

Time: 3 weeks

Activity: Students will have two weeks to learn about the problem and gather materials and information they will use to teach others. Then they will have one week to create an education exhibition for their community education project that will need to be displayed for others to look at and learn from.

Lesson: Begin with a YouTube video highlighting the problem in Zambia. This can lead to a discussion about the book and how Steve and Anna are building an education center with their own money and their reasons for this.

- Video: "Zambia Battling to Protect Elephant Population From Poachers" by CGTN Africa: https://www.youtube.com/watch?v=9t3dflCQKBU
- Steve and Anna's Chipembele Wildlife Education Trust: http://www.chipembele.org
- Elefence International: http://www.elefence.org
- Bulu: African Wonder Dog: http://www.buluafricanwonderdog.com

Using Steve and Anna's experiences building their conservation education center, as a class, begin a discussion about what students can do to better their own community through education. Let this lead into suggestions for community education projects that students can engage in.

Encourage students not to limit their research to the Internet, but also to contact people who are involved with the problem.

Once the student project has been approved, make sure to check in with students periodically to be sure things are going smoothly.

Meaningful Community Education Projects:

- Pollution
- Recycling
- Drug abuse
- Abuse
- Runaways
- Homelessness
- Hunger
- Bullying
- Dyslexia
- Autism
- Conservation

Figure 12. Sample project-based learning project related to *Bulu*.

In order to make the project even more authentic, the final assessment could put the project in the real world: Students could display their final product at an after-school presenters' fair of their own. You can invite other teachers and students, administrators, parents, members of the local government or school board, local nonprofit organizations, reporters, senior citizens, etc.

You could give this project to 25 different students and get 25 very different service education projects, but all of them would be authentic in nature because they are linked to something actually occurring in the world.

WHAT DOES A PROJECT-BASED LEARNING CLASSROOM LOOK LIKE?

Like most authentic learning, a project-based learning classroom will look very different than a traditional setting—the teacher in front of the class speaking to students who are sitting in seemingly permanent rows of desks. Because students are often working independently of the teacher during PBL, the classroom needs to provide students space. A PBL classroom might look like Figure 13.

Notice that there are three configurations in the classroom, all three of which might be used for a daily PBL class. The class might begin with the students sitting in the chairs in conference room formation, pointed at the LCD screen. This way the teacher can begin with instruction or direction for what the day should bring. This would not be more than 10 minutes of time and might be an introduction of the project, a new skill, or just a reminder of students' learning target or when the deadline for the project is approaching. Afterward, if students are collaborating, they can use one of the three tables at the back of the room. The chairs from the conference room formation can easily be moved to the tables on a needed basis. This allows groups to have discussions about the progress of their projects and gives them space to problem solve together. Finally, there are individual desks that border the classroom. Students can move their chairs so they have their own personal space to work if need be. Think of these areas as students' own cubicles so that they can work on whatever task the project requires of them. This might mean spreading out on the floor or going out into the hallway to provide more space to work. This flexible seating allows students to put themselves in an environment that will best enable them to complete their project.

Notice where the teacher desk is—the middle of the classroom. This is because the role of the teacher is to observe students' process and progress as they work on

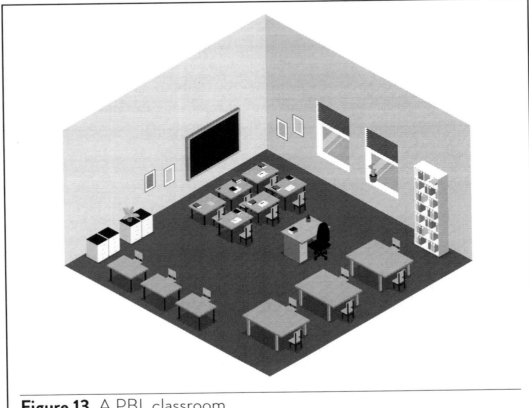

Figure 13. A PBL classroom.

their projects. What better way to do that than by being in the center of the room? Many teachers put their desks in the corner. This cuts students off from approaching the teacher. It acts as a border between their space and the teacher's space. Setting the teacher desk in the middle of the room makes for a more inviting environment where students have easy access to the teacher as a resource.

ADVANTAGES OF PROJECT-BASED LEARNING

According to the Buck Institute for Education (2018), research studies have demonstrated that project-based learning can:

- be more effective than traditional instruction in increasing academic achievement on annual state-administered assessment tests.

- be more effective than traditional instruction for teaching mathematics, economics, science, social science, clinical medical skills, and for careers in the allied health occupations and teaching.
- be more effective than traditional instruction for long-term retention, skill development and satisfaction of students and teachers.
- be more effective than traditional instruction for preparing students to integrate and explain concepts.
- improve students' mastery of 21st-century skills.
- be especially effective with lower-achieving students.
- provide an effective model for whole school reform. (para. 1)

In addition, project-based learning is great for high-ability students because it naturally differentiates. This is because with project-based learning, students:

- can go as deep as they want into a project;
- are self-paced, so they do not have to wait for the rest of the class to catch up;
- can use existing skills and knowledge in any way they choose;
- have the chance to use creative as well as academic ability; and
- gain the confidence to become lifelong learners.

STEPS TO PROJECT-BASED LEARNING

How does one create a project, much less an authentic one? There are six steps to creating a project:

1. Define the problem.
2. Develop solution options.
3. Plan the project.
4. Execute the plan.
5. Monitor and control progress.
6. Close project.

You begin by defining the problem. This should be an authentic, real-world issue. Take, for example, our community education project based on *Bulu*. The idea of educating your community about a difficult problem is authentic. By focusing the project on something that is authentic, students make connections to the real world and understand the context of what they are learning.

Authentic Learning

Another way to make the project authentic is by having an authentic solution option. If you have students learn about addition and subtraction of money by answering questions on a worksheet, that is not particularly authentic. If, however, the lesson required students to accompany a parent to the grocery store and keep track of how much selected items cost, how much money will be needed to pay for them, and what the change from that money would be, students would benefit from a couple of authentic experiences: (1) seeing how much things cost and determining change in a real-life situation and (2) going to the grocery store. Some students do not really think about how food gets in their house. It just seems to appear. Actually seeing what goes into the buying of these materials and the context of a budget would be a valuable experience for them to have.

Once you have decided on an authentic problem and solution option, you must plan the project. The best way to plan for a long-term project is to start at the end. What do you want students to be able to produce at the end of the project? What would show that they have mastered the skill you intended them to? This is known as backward building (Wiggins & McTighe, 2005):

- Identify what you want to *accomplish*.
- Determine the *product* that will show what you learned.
- Plan how you will *develop* this product.

Figure 14 shows what this would look like for the service education project based on *Bulu*. There are some aspects that could be added, such as a debriefing after the guest presenters' fair to discuss what students saw, or a debriefing at the end of the project to get a sense of what students got out of the experience. There are also aspects that could be pulled out. If your students already understand how to conduct research, that lesson will not be necessary. Similarly, if students have given several presentations in your class already, you might not need to spend an entire lesson going over that. There is one thing to consider, however: Do not assume your students have these skills. If they have displayed them to you in the past, then this can act as your preassessment, but if you assume that because of past schooling they already possess these skills, you might be surprised.

Executing the plan means gathering all of the necessary resources for students to participate in the project. This would include arranging speakers for the presenters' fair, making sure students have Internet access for conducting research, and carving out time for students to practice their presentations. Monitoring and controlling progress means checking in with students every once in a while to make sure they are on the right track. The more space you give students, however, the more independence

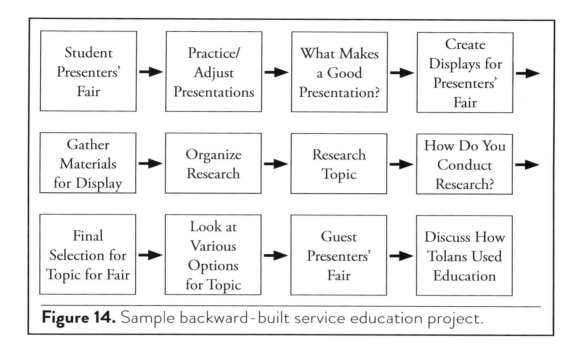

Figure 14. Sample backward-built service education project.

you are creating in them and the more initiative they will have to undertake. This is where that spectrum of teacher-led versus student-led comes into play (see p. 61). As the teacher, you need to gauge how much managing you will need to do without micromanaging the project for students. The final step is closing the project using a debriefing or reflection. Oftentimes, we do not provide students with the time or opportunity to adequately reflect, but it is so important to enduring learning. You have to be purposeful about this reflection and not just go onto the next unit before students truly understand what they learned from the last one.

KEEPING IT AUTHENTIC

There are many projects already out there that you can employ for your lessons. You need not reinvent the wheel. However, if you are going to ensure the project is authentic, you need to make it specific to your students and make a connection from them to the real world.

Just the act of working on a project is in itself an authentic task. Life is all about working on projects. From tending the yard, to cooking a meal, to planning a vacation, to creating a presentation for one's boss, these are projects where one must employ task

Authentic Learning

prioritization and time management in order to be successful. These are the very same skills one learns while working on a project and can be applied to the life of the student. Skehan (1998) outlined the most important life skills that project work provides:

> Project work enables the gradual development of autonomy with progressively greater responsibility being taken by learners . . . [Project work] is an excellent structure for preparing learners to approach learning in their own way, suitable to their own abilities, styles, and preferences. (p. 273)

If that is not a lifelong learner, I am not sure what is.

7 Chapter

Problem-Based Learning

> There is no end to education. It is not that you read a book, pass an examination, and finish with education. The whole of life, from the moment you are born to the moment you die, is a process of learning.
> —Jiddu Krishnamurti

Although they share a lot of similarities, the biggest distinction between project-based learning and problem-based learning (PrBL) is that problem-based learning is more about *the process*, not the final product. In a project, students work toward an end goal—a product that answers the essential question. This might be a presentation, an assessment, a display, or another performance-based assessment. Problem-based learning is not about the final aspect—it is what you did to get there.

Process is very underrated in education. Some teachers determine sole credit based on whether a student's answer is either right or wrong. There is no evaluation of how hard the student worked, how many ways he or she attempted the answer, what techniques were employed, or what successes he or she encountered along the way before reaching a final answer. As we know, in life, the process is far more important than the final result. For example, consider a professional football game. The team does not just show up on Sunday to play the game. There are several processes that go into that game. The coaches and players will analyze film of the other team to look for trends. The coaches draw up plays designed to expose weaknesses in the other team as well as play to their own team's strengths. The team practices, which is a form of process, and players learn what they need to do in order to be successful. The equipment manager has to make sure everyone has the proper equipment in order to compete, and the trainer needs to make sure everyone is healthy enough to contribute. There are several processes that go into that final product on Sunday. Without these processes, the team will lose and lose badly. In most cases, the better-prepared teams are those that are successful. The New England Patriots, love them or hate them, for the past 10 years, have been one of the better teams in football. It certainly helps to have Tom Brady as a quarterback, but the key to the team's success is that the coach, Bill Belichick, is one of the most prepared coaches in the league. He is going to work harder than any other coach on the processes. He makes sure to get players on his team who have a similar preparation and coaches who can prepare them. Are there times the Patriots practice really hard in a given week and end up losing the game? Yes, it happens. And the team is evaluated only on the result, which is not where the learning takes place. The learning takes place during the process.

In many cases, students only reflect when they receive less than an A. If a student got a B, he looks at the cause of this and tries to fix it or not repeat it the next time. For example, maybe he made some spelling errors in a research paper because he only used the spell check and it did not correct homophones incorrectly used. He will hopefully remind himself the next time to proofread the paper in addition to the spell check. If he left out certain details that caused the paper to be given a C, he might look back at his notes and realize they were very sparse, and thus he had nothing with which to create the details. The next time he will make sure to take more extensive notes in order to achieve the quality of detail being looked for.

Students can even learn a lot even when they receive a failing grade. It would seem, in fact, the only thing they learned was from the process. The most important lesson they might learn is what not to do during the process in order to end up with the bad grade. What could have been changed during the process in order to achieve a better outcome? Maybe they did not have good time management and missed deadlines. Maybe they did not pay attention to the requirements of the project and thus left important aspects out. Maybe they chose to fail. Even if that is the case, it is important for the student to understand it was a choice, and by making other choices, a different result would have occurred.

Even if a student receives an A for an assignment, he or she needs to reflect on the process to understand what had to happen in order to receive the grade. Through this reflection, the student learns to repeat successful aspects of the process in order to succeed on the next assignment. Some parts of the process might be different, but if the student learns how to successfully use the 21st-century skills discussed in Chapter 2, he or she can adapt to the process and get similar results. In forthcoming assignments, the student might employ strategies like good study habits, the use of particular websites or search engines that were helpful, asking a parent to look over the assignment before it is handed in, or understanding what the expectations of the teacher are. If the student does not understand why he or she got the A, a golden opportunity for authentic learning has passed. He or she will not be able to retain the blueprint for how to get a successful grade in that class.

WHAT IS PROBLEM-BASED LEARNING?

We do a lot of problem solving in our lifetimes. We solve problems every minute of every day, from large-scale problems, such as affording your child's college tuition, to the most tedious problems, such as how to open a stubborn jar of spaghetti sauce. Problem solving, in many cases, is arriving at a decision based on prior knowledge and reasoning. In the case of college tuition, you might reflect upon your own experiences and what you needed to do in order to get your tuition paid. For the spaghetti jar, it might be finding the strongest person in the house because he had opened difficult jars in the past.

During the problem-solving process, you may come to the conclusion that you need to get additional information you do not possess in order to solve the problem. This is recognition of a need to learn. This is what problem-based learning is. For the college tuition scenario, maybe you did not go to college, so to get some ideas, you speak with friends or family members who sent their child to college. Or Dad is not home to open the spaghetti jar, so you go online and find a video where someone uses a towel for more leverage to open it. The heart of problem-based learning is this need to learn in order to solve a problem.

The biggest difference between problem solving and PrBL is with whom the knowledge lies. In other words, when problem solving, the teacher is the content expert. She will indicate whether the answer is right or not, and if it is not, many times will provide the correct one. She might also provide the resources the student will need to solve the problem. In PrBL, the student is the one who is checking his or her answer to see if what he or she has hypothesized is correct. The control lies with him or her as how to go about finding out the knowledge required in order to answer the question.

Authentic Learning

HOW IS PROBLEM-BASED LEARNING AUTHENTIC?

PrBL is authentic if the problem is authentic. If you give a student a math problem that has no real-world context to it (e.g., "What is 2 + 2?"), the problem is being solved in a vacuum. Students cannot see where the learning fits into their own lives, other than being told it does. However, what if the problem becomes real world, such as, "You have 2 gumballs, and you get 2 more gumballs. How many gumballs do you have in total?" First, who would not want more gumballs? Second, now the students can visualize this problem in a real-world context. There are hundreds of math problems we encounter daily in our lives. Yet how many teachers present math in a real-world, authentic situation?

An example of authentic problem-based learning might relate to a standard included in the Common Core State Standards for Mathematics, such as 5.MD.C.5, which reads (National Governors Association Center for Best Practices & Council of Chief State School Officers, 2010):

> Relate volume to the operations of multiplication and addition and solve real world and mathematical problems involving volume.

A teacher could create a problem where students determine the volume of a bathtub. The students might be provided with a worksheet that includes an illustration of the bathtub and its dimensions. With this information, students are likely to arrive at the same correct answer. But how much more significant and meaningful to the students would the problem be if the teacher charged them with finding out the volume of their own bathtubs? Students would have to do some research on their own. They would have to figure out the measurements of their tubs. In the real world, bathtubs are rarely perfectly square, which would present an additional challenge. Students would have to factor in the curvature of the tub, the possible varying depths, and other real-world problems we often cannot capture on a piece of paper. Because 25 students will have 25 different types of tubs, the final results are going to vary from student to student. However, teachers can evaluate the process that students employed in order to find the measurements and how they translated those dimensions into the volume.

Problems can be set up similarly in other areas. Students might read about current events and then debate them to explore nonfiction text in language arts class, conduct experiments of their own creation using the scientific method in science class, or try to develop practical solutions to solve global problems in almost any class. All of these examples combine problem solving with authentic learning.

WHAT DOES A PROBLEM-BASED CLASSROOM LOOK LIKE?

PrBL looks very different than the traditional classroom. Traditional learning usually follows the process illustrated in Figure 15. The process of problem-based learning, on the other hand, looks more like Figure 16. The first step in both of these processes involves the teacher. However, by the time you get to the second and third step of PrBL, the process is in the control of the student, making the learning authentic.

In the classroom, this might look like the following:

> **Problem:** The school's student council has decided to raise money to offer relief to people recovering from an earthquake in Mexico. In order to do this, the council has asked each homeroom to create and sell a product at the school's meet-the-teacher night. There will be hundreds of parents in attendance, so it will be a good opportunity to have some customers. Your class needs to decide what product it is going to make, as well as how to advertise and market the product so that people are aware they can buy it. The proceeds from the sales will go toward disaster relief efforts in Mexico.

This is Step 1 of the process presented in Figure 16. Students have been presented with a problem. In this case, it does not come directly from the teacher but rather the student council. Regardless, the problem is generated by someone other than the students trying to solve it. Step 2 involves the homeroom working together in order to make a choice. What will the product be? How can it be marketed? What are examples students have seen in the past? These are all questions generated and answered by the students through research and experience. One student might share how she was at the county fair, and snow cones were a big hit. Another might point out that the class should sell Christmas-themed products because this event is a couple of weeks before the holiday, and it would be easier to market. This might involve taking a survey of potential customers to determine what they want.

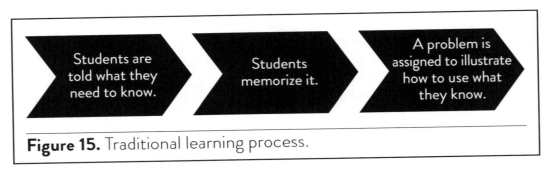

Figure 15. Traditional learning process.

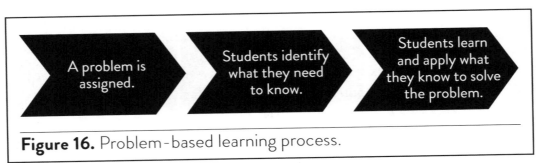

Figure 16. Problem-based learning process.

Once the students have made these decisions, they will decide how they intend to carry out their plan. What materials will be needed? How will labor be divided? Who is responsible for bringing in supplies? Who will fund the materials you need? How will you set the price in order to make money? What will your advertising look like? Students will research and learn so that they can apply this knowledge in order to make a product that will sell well and make money for the people of Mexico. This might involve looking at existing advertisements and seeing what draws the attention of people. Or it could involve scoping out the best place to post a sign or the selling table in order for more people to see it during the meet-the-teacher night. The students are the ones answering the questions and driving the learning.

ADVANTAGES TO PROBLEM-BASED LEARNING

The obvious advantage to problem-based learning is that life is one very large problem-based learning experience. If you are good at problem solving, especially practical problem solving, you will have a very successful career and life. According to Loudenback (2016), these are the top 10 jobs for people who love to solve problems, along with their salaries:

1. Government-property inspector or investigator ($55,000)
2. Sports medicine physician ($197,000)
3. Neurologist ($197,000)
4. Radiologist ($197,000)
5. Nurse anesthetist ($160,000)
6. Air-traffic controller ($118,000)
7. Anesthesiologist ($250,000)
8. Ophthalmologist ($197,000)
9. Judge ($116,000)
10. Chief executive ($185,000)

It should be noted that out of the 10 jobs, nine of them pay in the six-figure range. Problem solving is a skill that is highly valued in the business world.

In the end, students are able to learn for themselves. They do not need someone to direct them in the right direction or someone to check on their work all of the time. Instead, students learn to take initiative and seek to solve the problem, rather than waiting for someone to point out the solution. Businesses seek these learners. According to Hansen and Hansen (2018), these are the top 14 skills businesses are looking for from prospective employees:

1. professionalism,
2. honesty and integrity,
3. adaptability,
4. problem solving,
5. responsibility,
6. loyalty,
7. motivation of others,
8. self-confidence,
9. self-motivation,
10. willingness to learn,
11. leadership,
12. multicultural awareness,
13. planning and organization, and
14. teamwork abilities.

If you look at the list, many correlate with the skills problem-based learning teaches, such as adaptability, problem solving, motivation, self-confidence, self-motivation,

willingness to learn, and planning and organization. By using PrBL, you equip students with skills that will benefit them in the real-world workforce.

STEPS TO PROBLEM-BASED LEARNING

When using problem-based learning in the classroom, there are certain steps to go through. These steps are:

1. Present the problem.
2. List what is known.
3. Develop a problem statement.
4. List what is needed.
5. List actions, solutions, or hypothesis.
6. Present and support the solution.

The only step the teacher would be directly responsible for would be presenting the problem. From there, the teacher moves into a coaching role, making sure to monitor the remaining steps. Students might need some examples or models of problem statements in order to create their own. Here are some problem statements from various subject areas:

- **Social studies:** How might the world be different if the Roman Empire had not adopted Christianity as its religion?
- **Language arts:** What is the best way to convince someone of the value of reading the classics?
- **Science:** What effects has the discovery of DNA had on the world, both good and bad?
- **Math:** Why might is be a good thing to have an understanding of geometry in regard to the real world?

The teacher might need to meet with students to determine that they are on the right track with what they plan to present in order to support the solution. The most important role of the teacher is making sure to get out of the way and to subtly provide resources, support, or suggestions when students get stuck.

KEEPING IT AUTHENTIC

There are several key elements to problem-based learning:
- Knowledge and skills integrate across many subject areas.
- Students create a product that goes deeper than just answering a question.
- Not focusing on a single answer, students consider multiple points of view and perspectives.
- The role of the teacher is as the facilitator, with the students making the decisions and driving the learning.
- 21st-century skills are demonstrated.

All of these elements are important, but it is this last one that is most important:
- The focus is on content that is relevant to students and is a real-world scenario.

This is where the element of authenticity comes in. It is authenticity that allows students to make connections, and because of this, to care about what they are learning about. Authenticity will instill in students a love of learning in which they are active participants rather than passive receivers of information. It is this creation of the life-long learner that will benefit them for the rest of their lives.

8 Chapter

Case-Based Learning

I employ case studies of failure into my courses, emphasizing
that they teach us much more than studies of success. It is
not that success stories cannot serve as models of good design
or as exemplars of creative engineering. They can do that,
but they cannot teach us how close to failure they are.

—Henry Petroski

Case-based learning got its start in medical and law schools. The idea was to study actual cases in order to learn from them. By analyzing real-world cases, learning turned from theory to practice. Students would look at a case's successes and failures. They could look at a case involving a patient who died on the operating table and determine if a different course of action would have gotten a different result. Or students could analyze a court case to determine what defense was used and what was cited that resulted in the desired outcome. This allowed students to play the ultimate "What if . . ." game. What if they had been the ones with the patient or the ones arguing in front of the judge? What choices would they have made in order to be successful?

Authentic Learning

WHAT IS CASE-BASED LEARNING?

According to Ertmer and Russell (1995), case-based learning can be defined as:

> a teaching method which requires students to actively participate in real or hypothetical problem situations, reflecting the kinds of experiences naturally encountered in the discipline under study. (p. 23)

Notice a couple of keywords in this definition: One of those is *actively*. Students should be involved in the learning process. As mentioned, students who feel as though they are active participants are going to feel as though they have some skin in the game. Thus, their motivation to participate and succeed will be higher. The second significant word is *naturally*. This ties in directly with the authentic nature of case-based learning. This is not something that was conducted in a sterile lab, but rather experienced in the real world. More than that, a whole set of real-world consequences most likely followed. Students not only see how a situation occurred in the real world, but the implications of its happening. It is important to understand the context of decisions—that there is a cause and effect that might have long-standing, real-life repercussions. A lack of such context can leave students unmotivated to learn.

But what is an actual case study? A case study is a narrative description of a problem that comes from the real world of professional practice. It usually contains detailed background information and perspectives of those involved to make students more aware of the human element of these decisions. Cases should require students to have to analyze and think critically about the case (Carroll & Rosson, 2006). Cases are not usually cut and dry in nature. There are multiple possible outcomes, and sometimes, two different individuals making the same choice might result in different outcomes. Think of case-based learning as one of those Choose Your Own Adventure books. You could read one of those books dozens of times and get a different ending each time. The same goes with the case studies.

Figure 17 is an example of a case study that could be used for doctors from *Bouncebacks! Medical and Legal* (Weinstock & Klauer, 2011). Notice that the teaching points come from the errors. It is from the analysis of these errors that doctors in training would learn.

The question is: How can case-based learning be used in the K–12 classroom? In the example in Figure 17, the case could be used in a high school biomedical class to see the decisions doctors must make. In science class, it could be used to look at scien-

A 15-Year-Old Girl With Headache

Deep Thoughts

1. *Which historical factors are most important in the evaluation of headache?*
2. *Should we evaluate similar complaints differently when the patient presents per EMS?*
3. *How does the evaluation of headache differ in the pediatric population?*
4. *What role should "associated symptoms" play in the evaluation of a "chief complaint?"*

Part 1—Medical

The Patient's Story: Peggy is a 15-year-old high school student, usually to bed by 7:30 so she can be up at 5AM for school. She does not smoke or drink. She is one of 3 sisters, but is separated from her siblings and her parents; the other two sisters live with their father, and her mother lives in Phoenix, Arizona.

Peggy's home situation is unique; she lives with her grandmother, an engaged and caring person, founder of the Give the Children a Chance organization and host of *Gospel Dimensions* on WXYZ-FM. One of five grandchildren, Peggy has had some emotional issues, twice 'cutting' herself, one time placing multiple parallel incisions on the left forearm and another time eight on the left shin.

On the afternoon of September 11th, 2001, only hours after United 93 hits the ground in Stonycreek Pennsylvania, Peggy begins to cough and develops a headache. Her grandmother tries to get her into the car to take her to the doctor, but is unable—at 2:15 PM she dials 911.

At 2:20, the paramedics arrive to find Peggy sitting on the couch. They record: "Patient had a sudden onset of neck and head pain this am after coughing. Denies dizziness, nausea, vomiting, numbness/tingling of extremities. ABC intact. Is able to move her neck."

They transport and arrive in the emergency department at 14:43.

Figure 17. Sample medical case study. From *Bouncebacks! Medical and Legal* (pp. 73–76), by M. B. Weinstock and K. M. Klauer, 2011, Columbus, OH: Anadem. Copyright 2011 by Anadem. Reprinted with permission.

Authentic Learning

The Doctor's Version

The following is the actual documentation of the provider:

Chief Complaint: Headache

Nurse Note: Pt. c/o coughing and neck and head pains c/o stiff neck. Ears plugged—some nausea and vomiting of thin liquids. Pain scale 5/10

History of Present Illness (Per Physician Assistant, Ms. Kelly McKinney): Patient complains of throbbing frontal headache(s) for a few hours prior to arrival. No n/v, blurred vision, photophobia, numbness, fever. Patient denies it is the worst headache ever. No trauma. Stated it started after a coughing spell. The condition has remained unchanged since onset. There has been no reported treatment prior to arrival.

Review of Systems: Unless otherwise stated in this report or unable to obtain because of the patient's clinical or mental status as evidenced by the medical record, the patients positive and negative responses for constitutional, psych, eyes, ENT, cardiovascular, respiratory, gastrointestinal, neurological, genitourinary, musculoskeletal, integument systems and systems related to the current problem—are either stated in the preceding or were not pertinent or were negative for the symptoms and/or complaints related to the presenting medical problem.

The Errors—Risk Management/Patient Safety Issues

Risk Management/Patient Safety Issue #1:

Error: Poorly defined onset of headache

Discussion: When a patient presents with headache, fever, rash and confusion, my neighbor can make the diagnosis. The trick with headache is to find the life-threatening diagnosis lurking around the corner. Arguably the most important historical element in a headaches patient is the onset—and the paramedics did a more thorough job documenting this fact than the physician and PA. Special mention is required for the documentation "Patient denies it is the worst headache ever." A word of caution—this is a pet peeve of mine—more on this below with risk management/patient safety issue #6. Answers to the 'onset question' can vary widely. Often, a patient will say the onset is sudden only to mean that it started

Figure 17. Continued.

over a period of a few hours. That may be "sudden" in relation to the time span of their life, but certainly not our definition of sudden, reaching maximum intensity in less than 1 minute.

Teaching point: Every headache patient needs to have a clearly defined documentation of *onset*

Risk Management/Patient Safety Issue #2:

Error: Inaccurate documentation

Discussion: One of the most important aspects of the documentation is the general appearance of the patient. It is our Malcolm Gladwell's 'Blink' moment. It is our gestalt as we walk into the room; "sick or not sick?" The appearance is documented here but in a very general and nonspecific manner: "Alert and well developed. Age-appropriately oriented to time, place, 3rd person. Affect appropriate for age." To me, it sounds like it came from a computer pick-list.

Teaching Point: One of the most important parts of the documentation is describing if the patient appears sick or well.

Figure 17. Continued.

tific studies and the effect certain decisions had on those studies. In social studies, students could look at ethical issues, such as court cases like *Brown v. Board of Education* or the Dred Scott decision, and analyze how things could have turned out differently. English class could look at the use of texting and whether this has made students better or worse writers, or decide if Goldilocks was in the wrong for trespassing on the bears' property.

HOW IS CASE-BASED LEARNING AUTHENTIC?

Case-based learning is authentic because it bridges the gap between theory and practice. Consider the emergency room patient from the example in Figure 17. A medical student or practicing ER doctor could analyze this real-life case from *Bouncebacks!* and learn what to do if a similar experience occurs to him. Through the case, students are literally learning from the real-life experiences of others. Similarly, in the classroom,

Authentic Learning

if your case studies reflect real-world situations, students will be able to use these in order to learn what to do.

This is especially true with what are called "living case studies." These are case studies where the teacher throws in interventions while students are working on developing their solution. The rationale is that in the real world, often you do not have the luxury of studying a problem over a long period of time. You have to think quickly on your feet and be ready for the unexpected. Dieter Fink (2008) made an argument for the authenticity of this type of case study:

> Student experiences increased with a living case as shown by the diversity of tasks, the outcomes and ongoing feedback they received. For the usual 'static approach, experience to learn from the case study would be limited to a summative type of assessment. The emphasis on formative assessment with a living case supports constructivist cognitive thinking where students learn to learn as they learn. (p. 155)

An example would be a case study I did with high school juniors and seniors, where students had to create a budget in order to live on, including where they live, how they get themselves places, what they eat, and how they spend their free time. While students were researching for themselves and carefully make decisions, I would play a "life" card. This is something that might happen in life that affects your budget. It could be things like:

- Transmission on your car falls off: $500 to repair
- You catch the flu: $30 co-pay or $200 if you don't have insurance
- Your uncle dies and leaves you $1,000
- Taxes are due: $150
- You decide to adopt a dog; add $100 a month

These limitations would force students to have to problem solve and adapt, much like how the real world works. It is important for students to understand that no matter how much planning and research you do, something might come up to mess up the whole thing, and adjustments need to be made.

WHAT DOES CASE-BASED LEARNING LOOK LIKE?

The simplest case studies are the word problems you used to do in math class:

> Johnny is going to the movies. He has $20. The ticket to get in is $7. He wants to buy some goodies at the concession stand, but his mother told him he needs to have $2 left over for his lunch money tomorrow. How much money can Johnny spend on snacks at the concession stand?

Students are put in a real-life situation, and they must make decisions based on what is going on. These case studies can get more complex and involve more elements. Figure 18 is an example of a case study for a high school science class.

There are several different types of case studies that can be used in the classroom. You should determine which format is the one that is going to best get your learning objectives across and choose that one. Here are some various formats of case studies:

- **Discussion Format:** Students are presented with decision cases. They then must identify various issues and problems, as well as possible solutions. To aid in this, the instructor asks probing questions, helping the students to analyze the problem. For example, the teacher might introduce the topic of a government shutdown. Students would then research and identify some of the issues that led to the shutdown. Throughout the process, the teacher visits groups, asking questions, such as, "Have you thought about it this way?" or, "How do you think this group is affected by the shutdown?" Students work together to try and come up with a realistic solution to ending the shutdown, which they will back up with evidence.

- **Debate Format:** As the name implies, these are cases where there are two diametrically opposed views. The debate format could involve major current issues, such as abortion or the death penalty, or historical issues, such as the Crusades or prohibition. Each side is represented with arguments constructed by the students. In social studies class, this could be debating the shape of the new government after the failure of the Articles of Confederation. One side could be the Federalists making a case for a strong central government, while the other could represent the Anti-Federalists who wanted the power to remain with the state and local governments.

Chernobyl Disaster Case Study

Purpose: To illustrate how science both caused the accident and could have prevented it.

This case study examines the issues surrounding the Chernobyl nuclear accident that occurred in Pripyat in Ukraine on April 25–26 in 1986. Students need to consider the two causes of the nuclear accident and what could have been done to have either stopped or prevented these from happening.

Cause #1: During the testing of a turbine generator, the workers disconnected the technical protection systems, specifically the emergency cooling system. It is believed a combination of a lack of nuclear reactor physics as well as engineering led to this mistake. As a result, the reactor was being run with its key safety systems turned off. Might these systems have prevented the accident from occurring and how?

Cause #2: In addition to this human error, there were flaws in the reactor itself that might have led to the accident. The reactor had a large positive void coefficient of reactivity, which is very dangerous. A void coefficient is a measurement of the reactor and how it is affected by an increase in steam formation in the water coolant. Because Chernobyl used solid graphite to slow the neutrons down, it actually began to absorb the neutrons causing the reactor to become unstable even at low power levels.

There was also a problem with the control rods. These are typically inserted in the water to slow down the reaction. These particular rods were 1.3 meters shorter than they should have been. This space created between the rods caused the reactor's power to actually increase when the desired effect is to reduce the power.

Students should investigate both of these causes to first see if they are viable, and then to determine what could have been done differently in order to avoid the disaster. This will involve research to find out further information. From this the students will role-play what actions the workers specifically might have taken in order to avert the problem.

Figure 18. Sample case study.

- **Public Hearing Format:** This is a good format if you want to allow a variety of people to speak and express different views. A student panel listens to presentations by various student groups. A math class could set up a hearing on whether students should be forced to take math if they are not good at it. Several students could make their well-thought-out arguments for and against this statement with the student panel conferring on a decision from what was presented.

- **Trial Format:** Similar to debate format, trial format has the two sides, each represented by an attorney, and the courtroom proceedings are modeled with witnesses and cross-examination. You could reenact famous trials, such as the trial of Ethel and Julius Rosenberg, *Roe v. Wade*, or perhaps more obscure cases that may be more relevant to your course of studies. This mock-trial format is good for putting students into the shoes of others they may not otherwise be able to sympathize with. For science class, you could put Galileo on trial, with the prosecution trying to convict him of speaking out against the church, with the defense arguing that the Earth does, in fact, travel around the sun.

As the teacher, you want to choose the format that would make a lesson as authentic as possible for your students. For example, if you are a social studies teacher and you want students to understand the underpinnings of the Civil War, you could put Dred Scott on trial in order to show students all of the issues. You would then choose the trial format and conduct a mock trial, where students play different roles and create opposing viewpoints and arguments. Or if you are a science teacher who wants to have students understand the ethical dilemma of cloning, you might want to use the debate format, where groups of students would study and defend multiple viewpoints. There could be five or six arguments made, with each group formulating an argument and finding the research to back it up. Matching the format with the most effective way for students to learn a lesson will make a lesson as authentic as possible.

STEPS TO CASE-BASED LEARNING

Although there are many types of case studies, the steps students go through while learning are usually similar (Williams, 2004):

1. **The case is established:** This is an introduction to the case, which is usually provided by the teacher.
2. **The case is analyzed:** The student or group members begin to break down the case, determining what they already know as well as what new information they will have to find in order to be successful.

3. **Solutions are brainstormed:** The group collaborates to try and determine an approach to the case.

4. **Learning objectives are formulated:** Through their approach, students figure out what they are going to learn throughout the process. These become learning objectives, which can be assessed once the results are shared.

5. **New findings are disseminated:** Students combine what they already knew with what they learned together to create a product that encompasses their solution.

6. **Results are shared:** The results of the case study are shared with peers, parents, a panel of experts, or some other public forum.

7. **Students reflect:** This is where a lot of the learning will come from because not only will students reflect on the end results, but they will also reflect upon the process they took to get there.

As you can tell from the descriptions, the role of the teacher is as a facilitator. The teacher might kick things off by establishing the case, but a majority of the work is driven by the actions of the students, such as analyzing the problem, developing a solution, and sharing the results. The teacher might need to provide probing questions to help students gain a deeper understanding or to see issues from a different angle. The teacher might need to help students shape the learning objectives by providing examples or adding language so the objectives address higher levels of thinking. The teacher might want to provide a protocol for students to use in their reflections, especially if the students have not reflected often, such as a triangle, square, circle reflection:

- ▶ What are three points I will remember?
- ■ What is something I learned that squares with what I already believe?
- ● What questions are circling around in my head right now?

A good protocol can get more out of students and allow them to reflect more than just at the surface level. They can unpack the process and really determine what they got out of the lesson. The next chapter will discuss more about the role of the teacher when using authentic learning techniques.

ADVANTAGES OF CASE-BASED LEARNING

Because the goal of authentic learning is to create lifelong learners who possess a bevy of 21st-century skills, case-based learning needs to allow for an enduring understanding of the material. There are many research studies that indicate case-based learning allows students to study better (e.g., Dabbagh, 2002). Case-based learning also helps with the transfer of knowledge and expectations of the students from what they are learning (Sutyak, Lebeau, & O'Donnell, 1998).

There are many academic benefits that come from working on a case-based scenario (Barrows & Tamblyn, 1980; Mullins, 1995):

- Students sort factual data, apply analytic tools, articulate issues, reflect on their relevant experiences, and draw conclusions they can relate to new situations.
- Cases add meaning by providing students with the opportunity to see theory in practice.
- Self-study is used to consolidate learning that occurred in groups.
- There is an integration of both prior and newly acquired knowledge, leading to greater understanding.
- Cases allow scientific inquiry and the development of support provision for students' conclusions.
- Students seem more engaged, interested, and involved in the class.
- Because many cases are based on contemporary or realistic problems, the use of cases in the classroom makes subject matter more relevant.

There are also 21st-century skills that lend themselves to case-based learning. Some of these include (Merseth, 1991):

- analytic, collaborative, and communication skills;
- problem solving and critical thinking skills;
- active learning and collaboration;
- public speaking abilities;
- intrinsic and extrinsic motivation, allowing individualized learning; and
- self-evaluation and critical reflection.

Another advantage of case-based learning is that it addresses several learning domains. These domains include cognitive, affective, and psychomotor (Bloom, 1956; see Figure 19). Learners address affective skills through the experience of emotional reactions with the situation and the people affected by it through storytelling and

Authentic Learning

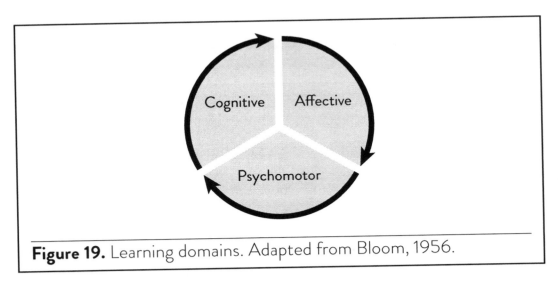

Figure 19. Learning domains. Adapted from Bloom, 1956.

researching the real-life event. Through discussion and problem-solving skills, the cognitive domain is addressed. Finally, the physical domain is addressed during experiments and hands-on activities. Put this all together and you get experiential or authentic learning.

KEEPING IT AUTHENTIC

Case-based learning is one of the more authentic teaching techniques because it uses scenarios from the real world. Students are not learning about some hypothetical situation or learning a concept they have difficulty seeing the larger picture of. They are learning about something that could happen to someone or actually did happen. These experiences are invaluable because the more of them we have, the better prepared we will be when we encounter them in our lives. It is sort of like writing. You can read everything there is on a topic, but you do not really learn how to do something until you experience them for yourself. The more writing you do, the more situations you find yourself learning from and the better you get at writing. How does one become a better writer? By writing. Similarly, how does a student figure out how to navigate the real world? By dealing with the real world.

9 Chapter

The Authentic Teacher

The best teachers are those who tell you where
to look, but don't tell you what to see.

—Anonymous

In order to have an authentic classroom with authentic learning, the teacher also needs to be authentic. What exactly does it mean to be an authentic teacher? An authentic teacher is *one who enables and inspires students to learn for themselves.* That means a few things that are contrary to the traditional methods of teaching:

- **Stay away from the front of the classroom:** A teacher should avoid talking to a class for more than 15 minutes at a time. That is all the time a teacher would need to explain to students the work they are going to be doing.

- **Avoid just giving information:** Teachers are usually considered the purveyors of information. They are walking encyclopedias, and they impart this knowledge to students by telling them about it. But in the age of computers, information is just a few clicks away, and these resources are far richer and authentic than anything the teacher can provide students. Rather than giving students the answers, the authentic teacher should help students learn how to find information on their own.

- **Don't do more work than the students:** In the authentic classroom, students should do a majority of the heavy lifting—much of the work the teacher would

Authentic Learning

traditionally do. This includes finding resources, making inquiries for possible interviews, and getting materials needed.

- **Don't be the sole source of evaluation:** Usually, students take a test or performance assessment, which is evaluated by the teacher. In an authentic classroom, the assessment can be completed by several sources, whether they be experts, peers, or self-evaluations.
- **Don't provide solutions every time you're asked:** Students need to struggle in order to learn. Part of that is figuring out things for themselves. If the teacher provided the solution every time a group or student struggled or headed down the wrong path, students would never learn how to resolve issues themselves.
- **Trust your students:** Oftentimes, it feels as though the teacher is the prison warden watching the inmates. Part of handing over your classroom to the students is trusting that they will do the right thing with what you have given them. Assume they are always doing the right thing instead of the other way around.

An authentic classroom can look very different from classrooms that most teachers are used to. If someone were to walk into an authentic classroom, it might seem chaotic. But creative work is meant to be messy, so let your classroom be messy at the same time. This does not mean giving up your classroom management strategies; it just means managing your classroom differently.

WHAT IS AUTHENTIC TEACHING?

What does it mean to be an authentic teacher? Kreber, Klampfleitner, McCune, Bayne, and Knottenble (2007) studied the literature on the topic and interviewed faculty and students. They found that a clear definition of *authenticity* was elusive, but they were able to draw a conclusion of their own:

Authenticity in teaching involves features such as being genuine; becoming more self-aware; being defined by one's self rather than by others' expectations; bringing parts of oneself into interactions with students; and critically reflecting on self, others, relationships and context, and so forth. . . . Authenticity is not just something that exclusively rests within myself . . . for authenticity to be meaningful it needs to be sought in relation to issues that matter crucially. (pp. 40–41)

These are all qualities we expect of our students in order to achieve authentic learning. It is only natural we should expect them of ourselves. The one that might be the most important is the "critically reflecting on self." As teachers, we can either teach one year 30 times, or we can teach for 30 years. If we are choosing to teach for 30 years, we are constantly changing our craft and trying new things. The next year looks different from the year before because:

1. **We become more experienced and thus more comfortable with trying new things.** When we are first starting out, we tend to stay inside the box for fear of messing up. The further we get into the profession, the more outside-the-box thinking we begin to do in regard to our teaching.

2. **We find our voices.** At first, we teach a lot like our cooperating teacher or teachers we had before, but eventually, we begin to learn our own strengths and weaknesses, playing to one while avoiding the other.

3. **New techniques and innovations are introduced all of the time.** Just like technology, there are new strategies being developed in the teaching profession, some having to do with integration of new technology.

4. **We are exposed to more professional development and collaboration with other teachers.** From these experiences, we hear something of interest to us and experiment with it in the classroom.

5. **We want to do what is best for students.** Once we realize we want to make a career out of this teaching thing, most teachers understand that ultimately we want to do what is best for kids. In order to do what is best for kids, we have to become better teachers.

In order to become a better, more authentic teacher, you have to be very reflective of your practice. This means admitting that things could be better, which is sometimes difficult, and improving them. The National Board Certification is a good reflective process. In it, teachers must create a portfolio, write about their philosophy of teaching, and "must also show they participate in learning communities and provide evidence of ongoing reflection and continuous learning" (National Board for Professional Teaching Standards, 2018, para. 3). You do not have to go through something as formal as the National Board Certification, however. Just the fact that you are reading this book means you are reflecting upon your own teaching practices and, hopefully, are finding ways to make them better.

Authentic Learning

PATHS TO AUTHENTIC TEACHING

There is no one correct path to travel in order to become a more authentic teacher. As long as you reach the end of your path, you end up with the following qualities (Weimer, 2012):

- being sincere, candid, or honest;
- being true to oneself;
- acting in the interests of learners;
- care for the subject; and
- ongoing critical reflection.

A tall order, indeed, but not impossible. If you are going to transform your classroom into an authentic one using one of the methods discussed in this book, you are on your way to becoming that authentic teacher. In your reflection of the process, however, use the above checklist to ensure you are being authentic as well.

How one transforms him- or herself into an authentic teacher might look like Figure 20. As part of that reflection process talked about earlier, the more teachers get comfortable, the more they can move their way up the pyramid until they have achieved authentic learning for the students in their classroom.

THE ROLE OF THE TEACHER IN THE AUTHENTIC CLASSROOM

As mentioned, the authentic teacher is more a guide from the side. Rather than telling students what to learn and how to do it, you are coaching them instead. A sports coach certainly guides from the side. You do not see a basketball coach throwing on his Chuck Taylors and jumping on the court with his players. A chess coach does not step over to the board to make the move for his student. Coaches help their charges by getting them as prepared as possible to face the challenges that come with their respective sports or activities. Similarly, as the teacher, you are preparing students to be able to function on their playing field, which will be the real world. You will be preparing them for this playing field because your classroom will put them in authentic situations they might face.

Figure 20. Authentic teaching. From *Defining Authentic Learning*, by S. Revington, 2016, retrieved from http://authenticlearning.weebly.com. Copyright 2016 by S. Revington. Reprinted with permission of the author.

In the authentic classroom, you take on this facilitator role, and you coach your students to reach their fullest potential rather than teaching them content. By coaching your students, you will (Stix & Hrbek, 2006):

- improve classroom morale and motivation,
- enhance an interactive environment,
- increase students' ability to resolve conflicts,
- encourage better organization,
- promote creativity and high-level scholarship,
- lower students' stress levels, and
- increase student productivity (p. 2).

All of these qualities are 21st-century skills that will benefit students well beyond school. What business would not want someone who can resolve conflicts, be orga-

nized, display creativity, and has a high level of productivity? Sounds like the ideal employee.

MANAGING THE AUTHENTIC CLASSROOM

Rather than direct instruction, the role of the teacher is more to manage the classroom. In order to manage his or her authentic classroom successfully, a teacher should follow these five tips.

1. Managing Stress

As an authentic teacher, you will have more time to individualize your work with students. Instead of teaching to a class of 30 students like they are a single entity, you can work with those 30 students individually. This means having conversations, making informal observations, and, rather than having one fix for every problem, being able to tailor the needs to the individual. The really nice thing about this is that you get to know your students. Even if you are a high school teacher with 150 students, you are going to know them a lot better in an authentic classroom than in a traditional one. Because of this, you will be better able to tell whether your students are getting overwhelmed or stressed and help them to manage this.

2. Giving Students Space

Because the teacher is not in the foreground, he or she needs to be in the background, close enough to step in should it be absolutely necessary, but far enough away so that students feel comfortable to work unencumbered. If students think the teacher is looking over their shoulders constantly and micromanaging their work, the end result will be stilted and less their work than the work the teacher has crafted. The following definition of good coaches and how they provide space describes perfectly the role of the authentic teacher (Stix & Hrbek, 2006):

> Good teacher-coaches are always patient, supportive, attentive, genuinely interested, and aware of what is important in a lesson. For this to be the case, coaches must remain somewhat detached from the activ-

ities at hand; rather than take ownership of the process, they should allow students to make their own way. (p. 28)

3. Keeping Students Focused on the Goal of the Lesson

One of the few drawbacks to conducting authentic learning in your classroom is, just like in the real world, students might not always keep their eyes on the prize. They might get distracted by the conversations, the tangents inquiry can spin off into, and the creativity of what they are producing. Even if they are the ones who created the essential question or the learning goals, they can lose sight of their endgame when they are in the process of creating. It is important to have a means to refocus student attention to what it is they are supposed to be learning. An effective way to do this is the use of a contract. A contract is a way of taking the grandiose and creative ideas students are working on, and funneling them into a tangible, concrete thing. An example of a contract might look like Figure 21. By setting essential questions, learning outcomes, and/or group goals, a student-teacher conference can act as the reference point to make sure students are staying focused. If you notice a student or group sort of losing their way, rather than telling them to get back on track, you can refer them to their contract, and they can figure out for themselves what they need to do to get refocused.

4. Conferencing With Students

You should conference with students when they are working on a long-term project, commenting on a piece of individual/group work, or reflecting on a lesson. When you are conferencing with students, using the authentic way, the student should be doing most of the talking about the process. Your role is minimal, at the most asking probing questions to dig a little deeper.

There are three types of conferences you can have depending on the needs of the students and the timeline of the work: status reviews, process reviews, and design reviews (Heagney, 2012, as cited in Stanley, 2016):

- Status reviews involve:
  - checking in with the group and making sure the members are where they need to be in regard to the calendar and deadlines;
  - the teacher and students sitting down with the calendar and seeing where exactly the group is throughout the process;

Authentic Learning

Contract

Student Name(s): _____ Due Date: _____

Topic: _____

Essential Question:

Learning Outcomes (At least three):

Group Goal(s): _____
_____
_____

Product: _____
_____
_____

Student Signature(s): _____
Teacher Signature: _____
Parent Signature: _____

Figure 21. Sample learning contract.

- □ informal verbal check-ins with the group to see how things are going or learning through observation where a group is at; and
- □ at least one formal status review a week, ideally in the middle of the week, so that students do not get too far behind.

- ■ Process reviews involve:
  - □ less about management of time and more about producing a high-quality product,

- asking two questions (i.e., "What have we done well so far?" and "What do we want to improve for the future?"; Heagney, 2012, p.143); and
- a meeting at the end of a work week or the first day in the next work week to reflect upon what students have to work toward their project.

- Design reviews involve:
  - the teacher setting aside time for students to evaluate their final products before the deadline; and
  - acting as a "rough draft or a rehearsal before the final performance" to see that any issues are resolved and that students are completing the highest quality product they can (pp. 71–74).

Here are a few tips for when conducting conferences with students:
- Listen.
- Listen again for understanding.
- Ask short, probing questions.
- Leave judgment out.
- Rather than trying to solve their problems, let them attempt to solve problems themselves, building capacity.
- If you do offer advice, keep it to one or two issues at the most.
- Make them show evidence to back up their statements.
- Don't let one student dominate the conversation.
- If a group seems like it does not need a conference, do not have it for the sake of having it.
- Leave the conference with a group plan for moving forward.

Some of the questions you might consider asking in a conference include:
- Is there a different way you could show that?
- How do you think you could make that better?
- What evidence do you have to prove that?
- What is your next step?
- Does that accomplish the group goal?
- What could you be doing better?
- What are obstacles that are preventing you from reaching your goal?
- Is the project going like you hoped it would?
- Does everyone understand their role in this?

5. Training Students in Group Work

This is something that is talked about at length in Chapter 5. It is important that you do the groundwork to help students to understand what collaboration should look like and, equally important, what it should not look like.

ASKING THE RIGHT QUESTIONS

In the authentic classroom, the teacher needs to make sure the questions he or she asks are ones that are going to further stir the pot of creativity and intrigue. Part of this is asking questions that do not have a definitive answer. Otherwise, once the student arrives at the answer, the discussion is over. What are probing questions, and how does one formulate them? Probing questions usually come from the higher levels of Bloom's (1956) taxonomy. The basic building block levels are knowledge, comprehension, and application. These usually have one correct answer and access lower levels of thinking. Questions at the lower levels are appropriate for evaluating students' preparation and comprehension, diagnosing students' strengths and weaknesses, and reviewing and/or summarizing content. The higher levels of Bloom's, analyzing, creating, and evaluating, allow students to use upper levels of thinking.

These are the probing questions used to spark inspiration in students and to make them think more critically. Some of these include:

- Analysis prompts:
  - What motive does _____ have . . . ?
  - What conclusions can you draw about . . . ?
  - What is the relationship between . . . ?
  - How is _____ related to . . . ?
  - What ideas support the fact that . . . ?
  - What inferences can you make about . . . ?
  - What assumptions do you make about . . . ?

- Evaluation prompts
  - Do you agree with the actions of . . . ?
  - How could you determine . . . ?
  - Why was it better that . . . ?
  - What choice would you have made about . . . ?

- How would you explain . . . ?
- What data was used to make the conclusion . . . ?
- Would it be better if . . . ?

- ■ Creating prompts
  - What would happen if . . . ?
  - What advice would you give . . . ?
  - What changes would you make to . . . ?
  - Can you give an explanation for . . . ?
  - How could you change the outcome . . . ?
  - Suppose you could _____, what would you do . . . ?
  - How would you rewrite the ending?

These types of questions encourage students to think deeply, help with problem solving, encourage discussions, and stimulate students to seek information on their own.

KEEPING IT AUTHENTIC

Ultimately, if you want to have an authentic classroom, you have to be an authentic teacher. That might mean changing a couple of things you currently do in the classroom. Why the change? Because if you are going to be expecting your students to be authentic learners, you need to lead by example (Revington, 2015):

> This new, authentic learning approach . . . requires another breed of educator. An academic as well as a life skilled, co-creator. A real, "life" long learner with skill sets and experiences that can facilitate a creative, diverse, well structured, team-based, open-ended, criteria based and globally directed education program. (sec. 3, para. 12)

This means asking the right questions, setting the physical environment, managing the classroom, and guiding students to be able to produce quality work of their own creation. By doing this, you will be creating lifelong learners—ones that can fend for themselves and thrive in the real world.

10 Chapter

5 Practical Strategies to Take Your Classroom to the Real World

> That's the beauty of education, kids taking lessons out of the
> classroom and back into their own world where they can positively
> affect their family, their friends, and their greater community.
> —Erin Gruwell

Going from teaching in a more traditional sense one day to switching to an authentic classroom the next is not a very realistic scenario. The change needs to be more of an evolution, where, as you are using more and more authentic learning opportunities, you are becoming comfortable enough with the process to transform your classroom into a full-fledged authentic one. In essence, you are becoming more authentic.

With that in mind, the next two chapters will provide you with teaching strategies that are designed to be authentic but do not require you completely changing the way you teach. These strategies will serve as stepping-stones to get you where you are ready to jump headfirst into authentic learning in your classroom.

Authentic Learning

There are ways to take your classroom to the real world by making the classroom a real-world setting, where students make real-world decisions with real-world consequences.

STRATEGY 1: ROLE-PLAYING

There is something powerful about having a student take on the role of an individual to try and solve a problem from that viewpoint. It offers perspective and context to the situation and allows the student to feel empathy for the individual, whereas otherwise there might have been detachment. You could have a student taking part in a debate on slavery where they play the role of a plantation owner. You could have a student role-play the character from a book and make an argument to justify the character's actions. In math class, students could take on the role of a number. For example, the teacher hands out a rational number card to each student. The students have to write their rational number in as many different forms as possible. Then, students have to make a giant number line where they order themselves from least to greatest. While doing this, students may talk with other numbers to try and figure out where their place on this number line would be.

Figure 22 is an example of how to use role-playing when teaching about the Greek city-states of Sparta and Athens. Rather than having students read about the differences in a book, creating a Venn diagram, or having the teacher just tell them about the differences, have them role-play in a competitive setting. Students will research their own arguments for why their city-state is better, backing up their perspective with a combination of common sense and research. Each student in the class plays a role, stepping into the shoes of a citizen from either Sparta or Athens. Students begin to care about how the city-states were set up because they are invested. They want to do well for their team, which motivates them. This is often how the real world works. Whether it be for family, a sports team, or work, when you support your team by investing your time and effort, what you produce is that much better.

Take Your Classroom to the Real World

Athens Versus Sparta

We are going to compare and contrast the regions of Sparta and Athens. The class will be divided into two sides, the Spartans and the Athenians. Each person will be an ambassador from one of the regions. He or she will have to debate directly with his or her counterpart about whatever it is he or she is ambassador of.

- Opening argument (introduction to the city-state)
- Education
- Military/Defense
- Government
- Citizenship
- Jobs
- Leadership
- Social Classes
- Commerce/Trade
- Law
- Philosophy
- Gender (male vs. female)
- Closing argument (sum up the city-state as a whole)

Situation: The Spartans and Athenians are going to fight the Peloponnesian War over who should control Greece. A group of ambassadors decides to present its case to a judge who settles disputes. He or she will hear both sides argue which city-state is more deserving of the rule of Greece.

- Divide the class into two sides and assign a task for each student.
- One will be the Athenians, the other the Spartans.
- Each side will debate which city-state was better and give examples to back its accusation up.
- Each student has the role of an ambassador and must play the role.

Worth 100 points:

- When students speak their part, they get a possible 70 points, provided they have evidence to back their stance and make a solid argument.
- For each additional point students make, they can get up to an additional 5 points but can only go up to 100 points.

Participation is a must. If you do not speak voluntarily, you will be called on, so you need to know what you are talking about. You also want to know about the

Figure 22. Example role-playing activity.

other civilization's subjects so you can compare yours to theirs and say why yours are superior.

- Example: If you have laws and you are from Athens, you will want to know not only what your city-state did, but also what the Spartans did. That way you can compare them.

Figure 22. Continued.

STRATEGY 2: SIMULATIONS

Simulations are somewhat similar to role-playing in that they involve taking on a real-world experience. With a simulation, however, the scenario drives the real-world learning. Students may or may not have specific roles in the simulation.

Figure 23 is a simulation where students must shop at a store, making sure they pay the correct amount, and understand what they have within their budget to purchase. In a simulation, students are put into a real-world situation, and they must use the skills they have learned and developed in order to be successful.

There are many benefits to running a simulation in the classroom, according to Pedagogy in Action (n.d.). Through simulations, students:

- **Actively engage in student-student or instructor-student conversations:** Students are active participants in anticipating outcomes and coming up with new questions to ask.
- **Transfer knowledge:** A simulation should include an extension to a new problem or new set of parameters that requires students to extend what they have learned in a previous context.
- **Understand and refine their own thought processes:** Following the simulation, there should be a strong reflection that requires students to think about how and why they behaved as they did during the simulation.
- **See social processes and social interactions in action:** Students see how the world works and interacts (para. 3).

Take Your Classroom to the Real World

Going to the Store

When you go to the store to buy groceries or clothing, everything you purchase is added up, discounts and taxes are factored in, and a total is given. Today, scanners and computers generally do all of this, but in this scenario students will need to determine final costs.

In this project, each student will simulate opening a store that sells specific items (e.g., clothing, toys, tools, etc.). He or she will sell these items, offering sales (e.g., 30% off or half off). He or she will be the cashier at the store, while classmates are the customers, exchanging money back and forth.

In order to demonstrate how this project works, the teacher should begin by modeling his or her own store. This can be done in a number of ways.

- Open a bakery. Students will shop using cards (depicting items) and pay with the play money provided. You will keep a running tab in the invoice. Once the store is closed, you will count up the money and make sure you have a balanced register, showing the math involved.
- You could provide students with play food or items brought in. You would need to price each of these items, and students would bring them to the register to cash out. Once the store is closed, you will count up the money and make sure you have a balanced register, showing the math involved.
- You could use this as a reason to provide a reward to the class (maybe they have just finished testing or a big project). You could provide ice cream with toppings or different types of pizza. The students would buy the items with the money provided (maybe some earn more than others). Once the store is closed, you will count up the money and make sure you have a balanced register, showing the math involved.
- You could go online shopping and, as a class, buy various items and determine how much change would be provided. Once the class has finished shopping, you will count up the money and make sure you have a balanced register, showing the math involved.

Figure 23. Sample simulation activity.

Abby's Bakery

Qty.	Description	Unit Price	Discount	Total
Subtotal				
Sales Tax				
Total				

Figure 23. Continued.

STRATEGY 3: MENTORS

Mentors bridge the gap between the classroom and real world. These are people who are out in the real world doing what students are learning about. Who better to know how to maneuver their way around the real world than people who are actually out there doing it?

Introducing mentors into your classroom can be done in a few different ways. Usually, a mentorship involves more than just one interaction. It might involve a few or even many over the course of the year. One type of mentorship is to partner a student with a particular interest in a subject with someone in the professional world doing what the student is interested in. For example, a student has shown a strong interest in being a veterinarian. Finding a vet who is willing to give a little time to tell her about his day-to-day work, answer questions from the student, and maybe even have her shadow him for a day or two, would give the student perspective on what being a veterinarian actually involves.

Alternatively, a content mentor helps students with something they are doing in school. If a student is completing a research paper on black holes, connecting him or her with a professor at the local university who is an expert on this content will allow the student to learn so much more than reading about it. Content mentors can use their expertise to help students achieve a greater, enduring understanding of an assignment or lesson. They can also put the content in perspective with the real world because they are putting the knowledge to work.

A third type of mentor would be one whom students can go to for advice concerning a long-term project. For example, if you have students competing in the Future City Competition, students are usually assigned an engineering mentor, who is in the field of engineering or who is an engineering student at a university. This person works with the students over the course of the year, going through the various phases of the project from the design of the city, the creation of the model, and the final presentation. Students can ask for advice, get feedback, or just run ideas past this mentor. This does require a longer commitment from the mentor.

Figure 24 is an example of a long-term project that involves the continued use of a mentor.

STRATEGY 4: INTERVIEWS

Imagine students could actually talk to someone who went through the Holocaust or who is an author of juvenile fiction books. Students would be able to ask this person questions, and he or she could share his or her experiences—experiences students can learn from. Unlike learning from a mentor, an interview is more a search for information and perspective. Because the person being interviewed has a unique skill or experience, he or she will be able to offer students a better understanding of what they are learning about. An interview also connects to the real world because students are not just reading about events and information on the Internet. They are talking with someone who has firsthand knowledge of a topic.

For example, in the project described in Figure 25, students are learning about different religions around the world. They will, of course, do their usual Internet research, where they learn the basic tenants of the religion as well as its history. The perspective of someone practicing the religion, however, will be more difficult to get from this research. That is why you can have students conduct an interview with someone who is from that religion, preferably an expert, such as a scholar or a leader. Students can even take it one step further and visit the local religious center of this religion, getting to see where people worship. An educational experience such as this would be 10 times more meaningful and effective than watching an interview online or reading one.

Authentic Learning

The Writer's Art, the Writer's Life

Overview

In this project, students will study the tools used by writers and artists to make a statement about the world around them. Students will explore the landscape of their own world through the lens of a writer, observing and listening for material, shaping experiences (both actual and imagined) into polished written pieces, and sharing and critiquing their own and others' work. The project will culminate in a portfolio of original creative work, as well as a public reading of each student's favorite piece(s).

Essential Questions

- How do writers and artists use the creative process to make statements about the world?
- How do writers use the world around them as material? How can you tap into your creative imagination?
- How do writers use a writing process (prewriting, drafting, editing, revising, publishing) to develop their best work?
- Who am I as a writer, and how can I translate my experiences (both actual and imagined) into powerful creative pieces?

Products of Project

Portfolio

Each student will assemble a portfolio of the best writing he or she has created over the course of the project. Each piece in the portfolio should be original to this project in order to reflect his or her growth and transformation through the project. The portfolio will include:

- a preface exploring his or her identity as a writer and transformation throughout this project (the preface also should indicate which piece reflects social and/or political commentary and talk about why the issue is important to the student); and
- a **minimum** of 15 typed pages of original creative work, including *three or more* different genres.

Figure 24. Sample long-term mentor project.

Workshop Participation/Peer Critiques

Students will learn about creative writing workshop protocols and will practice these with a small group of peers. Workshop will meet four times over the duration of the project. Students who are up for workshop will submit **eight typed copies** of their well-edited piece to their facilitator. Each student will have his or her writing critiqued twice.

Public Readings

Each student will present a polished reading of his or her own favorite original work to an audience. Students reading prose (short story, essay, etc.) should choose about two double-spaced pages to read; students reading poetry should choose two poems. Before reading, each student will invite a member of his or her workshop group to introduce the writer.

Mentors

Each student will be provided a mentor, a professional writer with whom he or she will work over the course of the project. Students can brainstorm ideas and genres with their mentor, run rough drafts by him or her, and have him or her help with a polish of the final draft or provide feedback on the public reading. Students can communicate with their mentor however best suits their needs. This would include Skype/FaceTime, e-mail, phone, or in person. Students should make sure they are respectful of their mentor's time by being prepared when they do meet with him or her. Students also might want to invite their mentors to their public reading.

Outside Learning

Each student is responsible for attending *at least one* writing-related outside learning opportunity during the course of the project. Examples of opportunities include: visiting authors at local colleges/universities, various monthly poetry readings, etc. To receive credit students must post a picture on the Facebook page of themselves with an author at the event they attend. Group pictures are okay. They also must add a few sentences to comment about what they learned about writing at the event.

Figure 24. Continued.

Authentic Learning

World Religions Project

Goals of the Project

1. To increase student knowledge and understanding of the major world religions.
2. To see how the religion has spread throughout many countries.
3. To compare and contrast religions with one another.
4. To have interaction with someone from the religion.

Standard Covered

Modern cultural practices and products show the influence of tradition and diffusion, including the impact of major world religions (Buddhism, Christianity, Hinduism, Islam, Taoism, Sikhism, and Judaism).

Product

PowerPoint Presentation that will include:

- **Section A:** Give the basic beliefs and traditions of the religion, including:
  - □ Geographic Origins
  - □ Founding Leaders
  - □ Teachings

- **Section B:** Use maps to show the origins and spread of your religion, including the major countries that currently practice it.
- **Section C:** Interview a follower of the religion you are studying. Through these interviews students will gain different perspectives for how the religion is viewed and practiced. As a group, students will present a written list of the essential questions and answers from the interview, as well as an analysis of what they learned.

Figure 25. Sample interview project.

Take Your Classroom to the Real World

Students do not need to be in high school in order to conduct interviews. Even elementary students can ask good questions if they take the time to prepare them ahead of time. If you are going to have students conduct interviews, it is important to teach them the professionalism of setting up an interview, in addition to being prepared with questions. For a face-to-face interview, students should:

- set up a time and place that works for the interviewee and the interviewer,
- bring a recording device *and* paper and pencil,
- be courteous,
- arrive early,
- listen,
- make eye contact,
- say thank you, and
- follow up with a thank you note, e-mail, or text.

No matter their age, it is important for students to write their questions ahead of time. They should then practice asking these questions to other classmates to make sure they sound like they intend them to. This scripted line of questioning will serve as the backbone of the interview to make sure students are getting what they need for their assignment, but be sure to encourage them to go off script, should a line of questioning take them there. For example, for the world religion project, a student might ask her interviewee, "How did you come to practice this religion?" The person responds that he just began practicing it a few years ago. A natural follow-up question might address why the change was made and what, if any, religion he practiced before. This will give more insight into what drew this person to the religion than if he just answered he was born into it because of family, which may not need a follow-up question.

STRATEGY 5: SOLVE REAL-WORLD PROBLEMS

Any chance you have for students to work on a real-world problem, the more authentic their learning is going to be. More than that, a real-world problem makes the work students are doing all the more important because the solution is something that could actually be used. For example, your school has a section of the sidewalk that is constantly submerged underwater whenever it rains. As a result, students have to traipse through the water, often getting their feet wet and tracking water into the school, which can be messy as well as a safety hazard because someone could slip on the wet floor.

What if you challenged your students to create a solution to this problem? They would have to brainstorm ideas for solutions, design what they come up with, figure out how to build it, gather the materials needed to construct it, and develop a presentation to convince the higher ups that their idea should be implemented. More exciting, what if their idea was actually adopted? How meaningful would it be for students to look at what they created being used every single day by their fellow students and community? How about 5 years later when they come back and see it still being used? This would certainly take the learning out of the petri dish of the classroom and put it in the real world.

Sometimes, these can be global problems. The Model United Nations program tasks students with finding problems in foreign countries and trying to find practical solutions. All of this should be research based. Students should find data to back up the assertion that something is a problem in the country, as well as find a viable, realistic solution that could be used. Figure 26 is an example of a resolution students wrote concerning the mine problem in the country of Somalia. There is an abundance of research located in the "WHEREAS" clauses that students had to find on their own in order to make the case for the problem they are looking at. In addition, because this is a problem the real United Nations might look at, the students decided to show how the problem not only affects their country, but also their region and the world.

For the solution to the problem, while researching, the students came across an article about how Cambodia has been using bomb-sniffing rats in order to safely discover and then remove landmines. Students found a real-world solution and applied it to the real-world problem. This solution might even be something the government of Somalia had never considered. Even though this is something that affects people thousands of miles away, students can get perspective on the problems in this faraway place and, more importantly, understanding of problems other than their own.

Take Your Classroom to the Real World

Nation: Somalia
Problem: The Safe Removal of Landmines

WHEREAS, over 1000 landmines and UXO (weapons that have yet to explode) reside in Somalia due to the Ogaden War and the Somali Civil War, and

WHEREAS, according to UNMAS (UN Mine Action Service) in 2011, anti-personnel mines caused 4% of deaths and injuries in Somalia, 55% were caused by UXO, and other unknown explosive items caused 32%, and

WHEREAS, in 2015, 887 people were killed in Somalia due to landmines, with 454 of them being innocent civilians, and

WHEREAS, in 2015, almost 50% of countries in Africa reported severe injuries or deaths due to landmines and UXO, and

WHEREAS, landmines are found in more than 100 countries including Iraq, Afghanistan, Angola, Iran, Cambodia, Mozambique, Bosnia-Herzegovina, Kuwait, Egypt, and many others, and

WHEREAS, of today, it is estimated that there are 110 million anti-personnel mines in the ground worldwide and another 250 million stockpiled in at least 108 other countries, and

WHEREAS, according to the United Nations only 100,000 mines are removed each year with current equipment, meaning it will take 1,100 years to remove all land mines, and

WHEREAS, yearly 26,000 people around the world are victims of landmines, meaning 70 people a day, and one person every 15 minutes, and

THEREFORE BE IT RESOLVED:

That the United Nations remove landmines using R.A.T.S. (Removing Anti-Personnel Traps Safely), a program that will use actual rats to detect and remove landmines as well as the following;

1. R.A.T.S. will partner with APOPO, a Belgian non-profit organization that has created an army of TNT-sniffing African giant pouched rats
2. Use these African giant pouched rats to help remove the landmines in Somalia
3. Start using the rats in other countries around the world that have problems with land mines after success in Somalia

Figure 26. Sample student-written resolution.

These rats have been tested in Cambodia and are capable of doing many extraordinary tasks;

1. They have removed approximately 13,200 mines in Cambodia alone
2. A single rat can search more than 2,000 square feet in 20 minutes, an area that could take a human up to 4 days
3. The rats are light enough so they don't set off the mines and are not harmed when sniffing them out
4. The cost to fully train one of these mine detection rats cost almost ⅓ of the cost it takes to train a mine detection dog

By using these specially trained rats, R.A.T.S. will be able to safely and efficiently remove land mines in Somalia and once proven successful, can be implemented in surrounding African nations and eventually countries across the globe.

Figure 26. Continued.

KEEPING IT AUTHENTIC

By using one or more of the strategies outlined in this chapter—role-playing, simulations, mentors, interviews, and/or solving real-world problems—you can gradually bring your classroom and students into the real world. Putting students into the shoes of real people through role-playing and simulations gives them practice for dealing with these problems in real life. Involving mentors and conducting interviews give students a direct line to the real world, allowing them to gain perspective and be able to receive guidance from someone actually experiencing what they are learning about in a classroom. Solving real problems makes student work meaningful because they are seeing their efforts being used for a practical purpose, rather than doing the work and seeing nothing except a grade. Exposing students to work that involves a real-world situation or person makes for an authentic classroom and closes that gap between learning and how the learning will actually be beneficial and used in their lives.

11 Chapter

5 Practical Strategies to Bring the World to Your Classroom

> To the extent that you can find ways where you're making predictions, there's no substitute for testing yourself on real-world situations that you don't know the answer to in advance.
>
> —Nate Silver

Ideally, we would take students out into the real world and let them learn there. That way, students experience the real world for themselves. Rather than look at art in a book or on a website, taking them to a museum to see art in real life would be a richer experience. As anyone who has seen famous artwork up close knows, photographs do not do it justice. Instead of telling students about the government, taking them to the state capital and having them experience the executive, legislative, or judicial branches in action would have a profound effect on their understanding of how it all works.

The bad news is that in today's day and age of shrinking budgets and liability, it is less likely that a teacher is able to pull off a field trip where students actually leave the

Authentic Learning

school building. Between organizing the busses, getting the permission slips, remembering the emergency medical forms, and going through the training to be able to distribute meds should the need arise, there are a lot of barriers a teacher has to overcome. The good news is you do not have to physically take students somewhere else in order for them to experience the real world. The world can be brought to them. With technology such as Skype, you can be taught Chinese by someone living in China. You can take a virtual tour of the Louvre without ever stepping foot in Paris. It is not just the advent of technology that can allow students to experience the real world, although that has certainly helped matters. There are several ways to bring the real world into the classroom so that students are getting these experiences.

STRATEGY 1: GUEST SPEAKERS

Guest speakers provide an excellent way for students to hear about the world firsthand and, more importantly, to be able to ask questions and explore further. There are three types of guest speakers you could bring to your classroom, all of whom would bring something more to the lesson than if a student were just reading about it.

The first type of guest speaker is an expert. For example, if you are learning how to build bridges out of toothpicks and you want students to understand the engineering involved, invite a practicing engineer to come and speak to your students. This person would use his or her expertise—expertise the teacher probably does not possess—in order to teach the students. Guest speakers can offer perspective on the real world because they are out there every day, living and working in it.

The second type of guest speaker is someone who has a unique experience he or she can share. For example, if you are learning about the Mayans and are talking about the temples they built, bringing in someone who has actually visited one or more of these and can share photos and stories from these experiences will be far more powerful than hearing from the teacher, who might not have ever been there.

The third type of guest speaker is a multicultural guest speaker. These are people who, by the simple virtue of being born somewhere else, can offer a perspective that others do not have. An excellent example would be foreign-born speakers. If you are teaching a unit on immigration, you can certainly look at interviews on YouTube, read firsthand accounts of arriving at Ellis Island from across the ocean, or hear an account secondhand through someone with a relative who is foreign-born. But imagine inviting half a dozen speakers who immigrated to the United States from a foreign country.

Bring the World to Your Classroom

They are going to be able to provide a perspective that native-born students would have no idea about. Not only that, the questioning can be tailored to exactly what the teacher and class are looking for.

Sometimes it is the age of the speaker that offers the perspective. Having someone come in and talk about what it was like when he or she heard that President John F. Kennedy had been assassinated or when he fought in the Vietnam War will bring a lesson to life with the speaker's stories and experiences.

It is important to do a little groundwork prior to a guest speaker visiting the classroom. Consider having students generate possible questions ahead of time. They can submit these individually, and you can pick the ones that would be best, while avoiding the ones that might be unintentionally offensive. Or you can have a discussion as a whole class, shaping the questions as they are suggested. These questions should be sent to the guest speaker ahead of time to give him or her time to prepare. Make sure to warn the speaker there might be questions not contained on the list, especially probing and follow-up questions that seek to get a better understanding of what is being talked about. Here are some other tips for how to get the most from your speaker (Cox, n.d.):

- Be sure that you prepare your students about the topic that the guest speaker will be talking about. You will want to challenge their listening skills, so it's a good idea to ask students to prepare a set of questions to ask the speaker.
- More than likely you are connecting your guest speaker with something that your students are learning in the classroom. If you are not, then it's important to do so. Research shows that guest speakers help build a link between academics and the expert. If you are doing a unit on food, then invite a chef; if you are doing a unit on the military, then invite a serviceperson.
- Make sure that after the speaker leaves, you debrief the students to maximize their learning. The more that you talk about what they have just learned, the more that they will benefit from it.

Where do you find these guest speakers? There are several places to look. You can begin the year by surveying parents of your students to see if there are any with specific skills or knowledge who might be useful as a guest speaker. Local businesses are another good source. You could contact a local bank if you need a speaker on finances, arrange for guests from an architectural firm to speak to students about design and construction, or invite people from the library who might be able to bring an added dimension to a discussion about a book the class is reading. Universities are usually very generous with helping find guest speakers. Depending on the size of the school, colleges typically have organizations, such as a multicultural center, which could aid in

Authentic Learning

finding speakers. Various departments often have outreach programs where they match up graduate students with younger students interested in topics, such as engineering, chemistry, mathematics, and art education. Reaching out to college professors to tap into their expertise is another route. Oftentimes, they are generous with their time and are willing to come speak to the class or offer resources.

One thing to remember: It never hurts to ask, as the worst that can happen is someone will say no. Once you get relationships built with these speakers, having them come in from year to year will be easier.

STRATEGY 2: STUDENT-CREATED MUSEUMS

Because taking students to the museum can be difficult or costly to organize, bring the museum to the school. Have students create a museum of their own, where they are in charge of the artifacts, displays, and exhibits. Each student or group of students should work on individual exhibits that, when put together, tell an entire period of history, an entire concept of science, or analyze an entire book. By doing this, students can become experts on their particular niche. So instead of 30 students getting a surface-level understanding of the overall topic, each student will gain a deeper understanding of one aspect and then share this with the other students doing their own exhibits. Experts will be learning from other experts. Figure 27 is an example of an Egyptian museum.

The added bonus to a student-created museum is that you can invite other classes to visit. This results in a few benefits. It gives the students creating the exhibits an authentic audience. Their displays are not just going to be viewed by their classmates or graded by the teacher. Other people, some of whom they do not know, are going to be coming and looking at their work. This authentic audience can cause students to produce a higher quality product because they want to make a good impression. The museum also exposes those coming to the museum to the information being displayed. They can learn by reflecting upon the exhibitions, just as they would if they went to an actual museum, but this museum can be better tailored to the curriculum because it is based on a learning objective. Depending on who you invite, the museum can also involve the community. Inviting parents for evening hours to the museum, seniors from a local retirement home, or school board and city council members, gives the exhibits even more of an authentic audience. This public exhibition allows students to talk to these community members and make a connection. The community members

Egyptian Museum

You are responsible for a certain aspect of Egyptian culture. You must create a display that visitors coming to the museum could learn everything they can about the aspect of culture. This means you will need an artifact of some sort, whether it be a model, poster, tri-fold, video reenactment, or some other. There need to be labels as well as an exhibit title. Like any good museum, you will need to have a sign that explains the exhibit in detail based on the research you find. Here are some cultural topics to choose from:

- Geography
- Religion
- Government
- Old Kingdom
- Middle Kingdom
- New Kingdom
- Daily life
- Pyramids
- Mummification
- Clothing
- Farming
- Class structures
- Pharaoh
- Gender roles
- Scientific contributions
- Hieroglyphics
- Art
- King Tut's tomb
- Cities
- Transportation
- Beautification

You can choose an aspect of culture not listed here as long as it can be linked to the Nile.

The theme of this museum is how the river shaped this aspect of culture, so somewhere in the exhibit this will need to be explained. Your exhibit will be evaluated on three aspects:

- Artifact/Display
- Content of Research
- Professionalism

Figure 27. Sample student-created museum activity.

benefit from seeing what students are doing in school. A real-life audience definitely makes the museum an authentic, real-world experience.

STRATEGY 3: VR GOGGLES/VIRTUAL FIELDTRIPS

Remember the View-Master from your childhood (or maybe you are not old enough to remember)? It looked like a giant pair of plastic binoculars that you peered through to see photos in a mini-slideshow. When you pushed down on the lever, it spun the wheel and advanced to another picture. You could change the reel and watch a whole different succession of pictures. The pictures were limited to 2-D, although sometimes if you got a reel that had a progression of pictures, you could flip through them fast enough to make it appear as though a dinosaur was moving or you were traveling through space.

Now that we are in the 21st century, there are goggles that work very similarly to the View-Master—only they are virtual reality (VR). Students look into VR goggles and are transported to another time or place. Some might explore local sites, such as a tour of the firehouse, a farm, or a park, while others are across the globe visiting the Great Wall of China, Chile, or the Taj Mahal. There are programs for swimming with sharks in the Great Barrier Reef, visiting the ruins of Machu Picchu, or walking through the Smithsonian Natural History Museum. You can even be transported back in time, watching Aaron Burr duel with Alexander Hamilton as though you are there, or traveling with the Vikings as they create a settlement and explore the world. You can watch doctors performing surgery, or explore the human body as though you are on your own fantastic voyage.

This allows students, especially those from lower socioeconomic backgrounds, to visit places they have never been before. VR goggles also give students an opportunity to go places they would never be able to go no matter their financial situation, such as Antarctica, the International Space Station, or the middle of an erupting volcano. Virtual reality opens up the classroom to the real world and gives students experiences they might never have. Additional advantages might include (Cummings, 2016):

- students become more engaged and motivated to actively participate in classroom activities;
- students digest and retain information at a much higher rate;
- students with different learning styles grasp what's being taught;
- students understand complex subjects in a way that's appealing and stimulating; and
- thanks to some VR platforms, teachers are able to track student engagement and performance in order to guide, observe, and control classroom activity and behavior (para. 16–18).

Bring the World to Your Classroom

You might think such technology would be expensive—and buying a top-of-the-line VR kit for a classroom of 10 can cost upwards of $4,000. There are less expensive alternatives, however. Google makes a cardboard kit called Expeditions (https://edu.google.com/expeditions), in which students can use their smartphones as their VR viewers in a cardboard holder. Students can experience virtual reality in this manner at a fraction of the cost.

STRATEGY 4: AUTHENTIC AUDIENCES

Typically, when students give a performance assessment such as a presentation, they are doing so amongst the peers of their class. These are the people they are interacting with on a daily basis, so there is nothing special about presenting to this group. What if, instead, an audience outside of the classroom was brought in to make presentations more authentic? After all, if you are facilitating authentic learning with authentic products as an authentic teacher, it would make sense to have the audience for your students be authentic, too.

An authentic audience (Burns, 2016):

- helps students connect their work in the classroom to the real world by taking student work out of a pile of papers (or a hidden digital folder) and placing it in the real world;
- provides a sense of buy-in for students and brings attention to their work;
- aligns with the Common Core State Standards, which have many standards that call for "a range of audiences";
- gives a purpose to students other than just presenting for the grade; and
- helps students learn "about the role of a school in a community and makes it easier for them to understand the collective duty all citizens have to support their school system" (para. 10).

Students write a ton of words on papers that are turned into the teacher, evaluated, and eventually end up in the recycling bin. Other than the grade, these efforts are not acknowledged or even have much of a purpose other than the student learning the skill being taught. What if you had students write to authentic audiences? Assign students to submit a short story to a literary journal for consideration of publication, create informational brochures about the dangers of opioid addiction and put them in the school office and city hall, or write letters to a pen pal or a soldier overseas. These are

all examples of how students can add authenticity to their writing assignments and create a purpose for their writing. This purpose will greatly influence their motivation and their adherence to quality because making a mistake does not just have the consequence of a lower grade; it might prevent an entry from being accepted or cause confusion.

Presenting to an authentic audience is also a way for students to step up their game. Having a panel of authentic evaluators rather than just the teacher will automatically raise the rigor because outside people will be looking for different things. If students are putting together a business plan, like a *Shark Tank* proposal, having local business owners visit the classroom to provide their perspective about what the business world is expecting would give students a real-world view. Or if you have guests come in to moderate small-group literary circles, focusing on a book they are passionate about, the conversations are going to be much more engaging.

Having a public exhibition is another way to have an authentic audience for students. When you hold the science fair, instead of just inviting parents, have people act as judges who go around and evaluate how the students do on their presentation. These can be other teachers or guests with some expertise in science. Host TED-like talks, where students have 10 minutes to present on something they are passionate about. Invite the community, the local media, as well as friends and family to make the event feel as authentic as possible. Other sources of authentic audiences are the superintendent, school board members, local politicians, and older or younger students.

STRATEGY 5: ACADEMIC COMPETITIONS

Academic competitions provide a level of authenticity. Because they do not just occur within the confines of the classroom with only fellow classmates to see the results, but might be presented to a local, state, or national audience or panel of judges, there is an increased urge to do a quality job. In addition, competition motivates students to rise to the occasion and produce better work than they may have had they not felt challenged.

A classic example of this is a spelling bee. Even in a world of autocorrect and spell check, the skill of spelling is something that is important for someone who wants to look professional. If you send an e-mail out to others in a professional capacity and use the term "weather" instead of "whether," which the spell check may not have picked up, the readers of this e-mail might cringe at this mistake. Not only that, there are

Bring the World to Your Classroom

links between the ability to spell and how it improves reading and writing, according to Joshi, Treiman, Carreker, and Moats (2008–2009):

> The major goal of the English writing system is not merely to ensure accurate pronunciation of the written word—it is to convey meaning. If words that sound the same (e.g., *rain*, *rein*, and *reign*) were spelled the same way, their meanings would be harder to differentiate. . . . The correlation between spelling and reading comprehension is high because both depend on a common denominator: proficiency with language. . . . The more deeply and thoroughly a student knows a word, the more likely he or she is to recognize it, spell it, define it, and use it appropriately in speech and writing. (pp. 8–9)

Students competing in a spelling bee can do so on a local, state, and national stage. The further you go in the competition, the stiffer the competition becomes and the more students will have to learn in order to compete.

MATHCOUNTS is an organization that provides engaging math problems to U.S. middle schoolers of all ability levels. Its aim is to build confidence and improve attitudes toward math and problem solving. Students work together on teams to figure out challenging math problems provided by the organization, such as "Three Little Piggy Banks" (MATHCOUNTS, 2017). The first phase of the problem starts simply enough:

> When Lucas dumped the coins out of his piggy bank, he noticed that there were only nickels and dimes, and the number of nickels was twice the number of dimes. If there were 50 nickels, what was the total value of the coins Lucas dumped out of his piggy bank? (para. 1)

But the second phase is more difficult:

> When Franco dumped the coins out of his piggy bank, he noticed that there were only nickels and quarters, and the number of quarters was six more than half the number of nickels. If the total value of the coins Franco and Lucas dumped out of each piggy bank was the same, how many coins did Franco dump out of his piggy bank? (para. 2)

Authentic Learning

And the third phase builds on the first two:

> When Callie dumped the coins out of her piggy bank, she noticed that there were only nickels, dimes and quarters. The number of dimes was one more than twice the number of quarters, and there were half as many quarters as nickels. The coins dumped out of Callie's piggy bank had a total value equal to that of the coins dumped out of Franco's and Lucas' piggy banks combined. What was the total value of the nickels and dimes dumped out of Callie's piggy bank? (para. 3)

This eventually leads to the students competing against others in problem solving challenges. Because schools are sending their best math students, individuals are facing stiff competition that causes them to raise their game and grow as learners. This is far more authentic than working on a problem by yourself, which is eventually turned into the teacher, assessed, and recorded in the grade book without any comparison to peers. This makes it difficult for students to see how math fits into the real world.

There are lots of different national competitions (see Table 2). The academic competition does not need to be a national organization. Having a local science fair at the school or holding a chess tournament for the district would still provide students with the authentic learning experience of competition with others in a real-world environment.

KEEPING IT AUTHENTIC

Using one or more of the strategies discussed in this chapter—guest speakers, student-created museums, VR goggles/virtual field trips, authentic audiences, and/or academic competitions—will bring the real world to your classroom rather than having to take students out into it. Not only that, using one of these strategies typically involves the community, whether it be local authors, university professors, parents with a special skill, business owners, or friends and family. This connects the students to the community and the community to the school, making for a real-world collaboration.

Bring the World to Your Classroom

TABLE 2

National Competitions for Student Clubs and Enrichment

Competition	Age Range/ Grades	Area of Study
American Mathematics Competitions (http://www.maa.org/math-competitions)	Grades 8–12	Math
America's Battle of the Books (http://www.battleofthebooks.org)	Grades 3–12	English language arts
Egg Drop Contest	Grades 5–12	Science, engineering
FIRST LEGO League (http://www.firstlegoleague.org)	Ages 9–16	Science, engineering
Future City Competition (http://futurecity.org)	Grades 6–8	Science, technology, engineering, math
Future Problem Solving Program International (http://www.fpspi.org)	Ages 8–18	Logic, global connections
Invention League's Convention Program (http://www.inventionleague.org)	Grades K–8	Science, engineering
Linguistics Olympiad (http://www.nacloweb.org)	Grades 6–12	English language arts
MATHCOUNTS (https://www.mathcounts.org)	Grades 6–8	Math, reasoning
Math League (http://www.mathleague.com)	Grades 3–6	Math
Math Olympiads (http://www.moems.org)	Grades 4–8	Math
Model United Nations (http://www.unausa.org/global-classrooms-model-un)	High school, some states have junior high	Social studies, global awareness
Odyssey of the Mind (https://www.odysseyofthemind.com)	Grades K–12	Problem solving, creativity
PhysicsBowl (https://www.aapt.org/Programs/PhysicsBowl)	High school	Science

Authentic Learning

TABLE 2, CONTINUED.

Competition	Age Range/ Grades	Area of Study
Power of the Pen (http://www.powerofthepen.org)	Grades 7–8	English language arts
NASA Ames Space Settlement Contest (https://settlement.arc.nasa.gov/Contest)	Grades 7–12	Science, technology, engineering, math
National Shakespeare Competition (https://www.esuus.org/esu/programs/ shakespeare_competition)	Grades 9–12	English language arts, performing arts
Science Olympiad (https://www.soinc.org)	Grades 6–12	Science
Siemens Competition in Math, Science, & Technology (https://siemenscompetition. discoveryeducation.com)	Grades 9–12	Science, technology, engineering, math
WordMasters Challenge (http://www.wordmasterschallenge. com)	Grades 3–8	English language arts, reasoning

Note. From *When Smart Kids Underachieve in School: Practical Solutions for Teachers* (p. 84), by T. Stanley, 2018, Waco, TX: Prufrock Press. Copyright 2018 by Prufrock Press. Reprinted with permission.

Conclusion

Now That Your Classroom Is Authentic, What Do You Do?

> Our rapidly moving, information-based society badly
> needs people who know how to find facts rather than
> memorize them, and who know how to cope with change
> in creative ways. You don't learn those things in school.
>
> —Wendy Priesnitz

The above quote encapsulates the problem with teaching traditionally in a 21st-century world. The world has moved on from teaching what you may consider is the traditional set of skills that every student needed to learn before leaving school. Each age has had a specific set of skills beneficial to those entering the real world (see Figure 28).

Unfortunately, some of our schools are still turning out students for the information age. Their focus is on knowledge workers. Teachers are tasking students to be able to memorize facts and formulas but not showing them how to create these for themselves. These students are leaving school with a disadvantage in that they are entering a job market that does not have high value in their particular set of skills. Interestingly enough, we knew about this shift in skills a long time ago, as evidenced in this quote from 1970 (Knowles, 1970):

> Under this new condition, knowledge is gained by the time a person is
> 21 and is largely obsolete by the time he is 40; and skills that made him
> productive in his twenties are becoming out of date during his thirties.

Authentic Learning

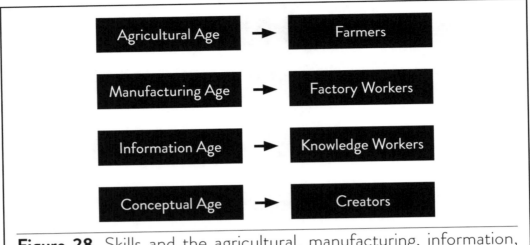

Figure 28. Skills and the agricultural, manufacturing, information, and conceptual ages.

> So it is no longer functional to define education as a process of transmitting what is known; it must now be defined as a lifelong process of discovering what is not known.

This quote is from nearly 50 years ago, before most of the teachers currently in the classroom were even born. The only difference is the speed with which the information becomes obsolete. It no longer takes decades. It can take only a year, or maybe even months. It is the educational system that has been slow to respond to this new type of learner. Now is your chance to be part of the solution rather than a contributor to the problem.

Figure 29 analyzes Wagner's (2008) Seven Survival Skills and the percentage of employers that seek those skills, according to the National Association of Colleges and Employers (2017). As you can see, nearly all of these skills are desired by 60% of employers. The good news is we have identified the skills we need to teach students. The bad news is it is difficult for students to acquire these skills if they are sitting in rows, being spoken at, or have their heads buried in textbooks. The way to learn all of these skills is by having a classroom where authentic learning is taking place. A place they are working on a case study where they have to find information in order to make a decision for themselves. Where they work on projects that allow them to learn to adapt to any changing situation. That means if you teach students these 21st-century

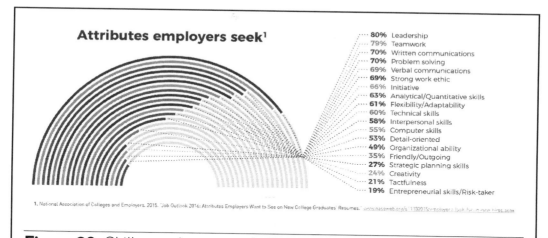

Attributes employers seek[1]

- **80%** Leadership
- **79%** Teamwork
- **70%** Written communications
- **70%** Problem solving
- **69%** Verbal communications
- **69%** Strong work ethic
- **66%** Initiative
- **63%** Analytical/Quantitative skills
- **61%** Flexibility/Adaptability
- **60%** Technical skills
- **58%** Interpersonal skills
- **55%** Computer skills
- **53%** Detail-oriented
- **49%** Organizational ability
- **35%** Friendly/Outgoing
- **27%** Strategic planning skills
- **24%** Creativity
- **21%** Tactfulness
- **19%** Entrepreneurial skills/Risk-taker

1. National Association of Colleges and Employers. 2015. "Job Outlook 2016: Attributes Employers Want to See on New College Graduates' Resumes." www.naceweb.org/s11920015/employers-look-for-in-new-hires.aspx

Figure 29. Skills employers seek. From *Employability Skills Fast Facts* by Pathways to Prosperity, 2017, retrieved from http://www.jff. org/sites/default/files/Employability%20Skills%20Infographic%20 1.23.17.pdf. Copyright 2017 by Pathways to Prosperity. Reprinted with permission.

skills in your authentic classroom, their ability to get a job in the real world is going to be much higher.

Going back to the quote that began this chapter, it ends with "You don't learn those things in school." What if that changed? What if school was the place children went in order to learn how to find facts or cope with change in creative ways? What if every classroom was an authentic space where students were doing inquiry learning in the form of projects, problem-based learning, or case studies?

You do not have to be the one to get things started. There are already teachers who have been using these methods for years, and there are more and more of them every year. Within the next 10 or 20 years, this is what all schools will look like. You have to ask yourself, do you want to be ahead of the game, or do you want to wait until it is forced on you by administration or the pressures of parents? If you have read this far, it is obvious you want to be ahead of the game. So pick one of these teaching strategies and begin to transform your classroom into an authentic one. Your students will be better off for it.

References

Autos.com Editor. (2013). *Car crash statistics based on age and location.* Retrieved from http://www.autos.com/driving-and-safety/car-crash-statistics-based-on-age-and-location

Banchi, H., & Bell, R. (2008). The many levels of inquiry. *Science and Children, 46*(2), 26–29.

Barrows, H. S., & Tamblyn, R. M. (1980). *Problem-based learning: An approach to medical education.* New York, NY: Springer.

Bloom, B. (Ed.). (1956). *Taxonomy of educational objectives: The classification of educational goals. Handbook I: Cognitive domain.* New York, NY: Longmans Green.

Bruce, C. (n.d.). *What is inquiry-based learning?* Retrieved from https://chipbruce.net/resources/inquiry-based-learning/defining-inquiry-based-learning

Buck Institute for Education. (2018). *Does PBL work?* Retrieved from https://www.bie.org/object/document/does_pbl_work

Burns, M. (2016). The value of an authentic audience: Providing students with an audience helps them understand why their coursework is worthwhile. *Edutopia.* Retrieved from https://www.edutopia.org/article/value-of-authentic-audience-monica-burns

CAP Immigration Team, & Nicholson, M. D. (2017). The facts on immigration today: 2017 edition. *Center for American Progress.* Retrieved from https://www.americanprogress.org/issues/immigration/reports/2017/04/20/430736/facts-immigration-today-2017-edition

Carroll, J. M., & Rosson, M. B. (2006). Case studies as minimalist information. *IEEE Transactions of Professional Communication, 49,* 297–310.

Cordes, C., Monke, L., & Talbot, S. (n.d.). Technology literacy: Four guiding principles for educators and parents. *Alliance for Childhood.* Retrieved from http://drupal6.allianceforchildhood.org/technology_literacy

Cox, J. (n.d.). Classroom management: Guest speakers support learning. *TeachHUB.* Retrieved from http://www.teachhub.com/classroom-management-guest-speakers-support-learning

Authentic Learning

Cummings, B. (2016). *Virtual reality in the classroom.* Ashford University. Retrieved from https://www.ashford.edu/blog/technology/virtual-reality-in-the-classroom

Curtis, D. (2001). Project-based learning: Real-world issues motivate students. *Edutopia.* Retrieved from http://www.edutopia.org/project-based-learning-student-motivation

Dabbagh, N. (2002). Assessing complex problem-solving skill and knowledge assembly using web-based hypermedia design. *Journal of Educational Multimedia and Hypermedia, 11,* 291–322.

Daggett, W. R. (2016). *Rigor/relevance framework: A guide to focusing resources to increase student performance.* Rexford, NY: International Center for Leadership in Education. Retrieved from http://www.leadered.com/pdf/Rigor%20Relevance%20Framework%20White%20Paper%202016.pdf

Delisle, J. R. (2006). *Parenting gifted kids: Tips for raising happy and successful children.* Waco, TX: Prufrock Press.

Dewey, J. (1938). *Logic: The theory of inquiry.* New York, NY: Holt.

Duckworth, A. (2016). *Grit: The power of passion and perseverance.* New York, NY: Scribner.

Ertmer, P. A., & Russell, J. D. (1995). Using case studies to enhance instructional design. *Educational Technology, 35*(4), 23–31.

Fink, D. (2008). Living cases: Authentic learning in action. In J. Renner, J. Cross, & L. McCormack (Eds.), *Proceedings of the EDU-COM 2008 International Conference: Sustainability in Higher Education: Directions for Change* (pp. 152–160). Perth, Australia: Edith Cowan University.

Friedman, T. L. (2007). *The world is flat: A brief history of the twenty-first century* (3rd ed.). New York, NY: Picador. (Original work published 2005)

Guido, M. (2017). All about inquiry-based learning: Definition, benefits and strategies. *Prodigy.* Retrieved from https://www.prodigygame.com/blog/inquiry-based-learning-definition-benefits-strategies

Hanover Research. (2011). *A crosswalk of 21st century skills.* Washington, DC: Author.

Hansen, R. S., & Hansen, K. (2018). 14 skills and values employers seek in job seekers. *Live Career.* Retrieved from https://www.livecareer.com/quintessential/job-skills-values

Jacoby, B. (1996). *Service-learning in higher education: Concepts and practices.* San Francisco, CA: Jossey-Bass.

Jones, N. (2010). Collaboration at work: A look at the pros and cons. *Bright Hub.* Retrieved from http://www.brighthub.com/office/collaboration/articles/73856.aspx

Jones, R. D. (2004). *Introduction to rigor/relevance framework*. Rexford, NY: International Center for Leadership in Education.

Joshi, R. M., Treiman, R., Carreker, S., & Moats, L. (2008–2009). How words cast their spell: Spelling is an integral part of learning the language, not a matter of memorization. *American Educator, 9,* 6–16, 42–43.

Knowles, M. S. (1970). *The modern practice of adult education: From pedagogy to andragogy.* New York, NY: Cambridge.

Kreber, C., Klampfleitner, M., McCune, V., Bayne, S., & Knottenble, M. (2007). What do you mean by "authentic"? A comparative review of the literature on conceptions of authenticity in teaching. *Adult Education Quarterly, 58*(1), 22–44.

Loudenback, T. (2016). The 20 best jobs for people who love to solve problems. *Business Insider.* Retrieved from http://www.businessinsider.com/best-jobs-for-problem-solvers-2016-3

MacKenzie, T. (2017). *Do you have an inquiry classroom?* [Web log post]. Retrieved from https://trevmackenzie.wordpress.com/2017/06/12/do-you-have-an-inquiry-classroom

Matchar, E. (2012). Can't find a job? Move overseas. *The Washington Post.* Retrieved from https://www.washingtonpost.com/opinions/cant-find-a-job-move-overseas/2012/11/23/b7322ef4-3273-11e2-9cfa-e41bac906cc9_story.html

MATHCOUNTS. (2017). *Three little piggy banks.* Retrieved from https://www.mathcounts.org/resources/problem-of-the-week/three-little-piggy-banks-0

McBean, B. (2012). *The facts of business life: What every successful business owner knows that you don't.* Indianapolis, IN: Wiley.

Merseth, K. (1991). What the case method offers the teaching profession. *Harvard Education Letter, 7*(2), 6–7.

Mullins, G. (1995). The evaluation of teaching in a problem-based learning context. In S. E. Chen, R. M. Cowdroy, A. J. Kingsland, & M. J. Ostwald (Eds.), *Reflections on problem-based learning* (pp. 105–124). Sydney: Australian Problem-Based Learning Network.

National Association of Colleges and Employers. (2015). *Job outlook 2016: The attributes employers want to see on new college graduates' resumes.* Retrieved from http://www.naceweb.org/career-development/trends-and-predictions/job-outlook-2016-attributes-employers-want-to-see-on-new-college-graduates-resumes

National Association of Colleges and Employers. (2017). *The key attributes employers seek on students' resumes.* Retrieved from http://www.naceweb.org/about-us/press/2017/the-key-attributes-employers-seek-on-students-resumes

Authentic Learning

National Board for Professional Teaching Standards. (2018). *National Board certification overview*. Retrieved from http://www.nbpts.org/national-board-certification/overview

National Governors Association Center for Best Practices, & Council of Chief State School Officers. (2010). *Common Core State Standards for mathematics*. Washington, DC: Author.

Oakley, B., Felder, R. M., Brent, R., & Elhajj, I. (2004). Turning student groups into effective teams. *Journal of Student Centered Learning, 2*(1), 9–34.

Pathways to Prosperity. (2017). *Employability skills fast facts*. Retrieved from http://www.jff.org/sites/default/files/Employability%20Skills%20Infographic%201.23.17.pdf

Pedagogy in Action. (n.d.). *Why teach with simulations?* Retrieved from https://serc.carleton.edu/sp/library/simulations/why.html

Reeves, T. C., Herrington, J., & Oliver, R. (2002). Authentic activities and online learning. In *Quality Conversations, Proceedings of the 25th HERDSA Annual Conference*. Perth, Western Australia: Higher Education Research and Development Society of Australasia.

Revington, S. (2015). *Defining authentic learning*. Retrieved from http://authenticlearning.weebly.com

Rule, A. C. (2006). The components of authentic learning. *Journal of Authentic Learning, 3*(1), 1–10.

Ryan, R. M., & Grolnick, W. S. (1986). Origins and pawns in the classroom: Self-report and projective assessments of individual differences in children's perceptions. *Journal of Personality and Social Psychology, 50,* 550–558.

Scharaldi, K. (2016). How to set the stage for inquiry-based learning. *Kids Discover*. Retrieved from https://www.kidsdiscover.com/teacherresources/how-to-set-the-stage-for-inquiry-based-learning

Simpkins, M., Cole, K., Tavalin, F., & Means, B. (2002). *Increasing student learning through multimedia projects*. Alexandria, VA: ASCD.

Skehan, P. (1998). *A cognitive approach to language learning*. Oxford, England: Oxford University Press.

SkillsYouNeed.com. (2011–2017). *Critical thinking skills*. Retrieved from https://www.skillsyouneed.com/learn/critical-thinking.html

Stanley, T. (2011). *Project-based learning for gifted students: A handbook for the 21st-century classroom*. Waco, TX: Prufrock Press.

Stanley, T. (2014). *Performance-based assessment for 21st-century skills*. Waco, TX: Prufrock Press.

References

Stanley, T. (2016). *Creating life-long learners: Using project-based management to teach 21st century skills.* Thousand Oaks, CA: Corwin.

Stanley, T. (2018). *When smart kids underachieve in school: Practical solutions for teachers.* Waco, TX: Prufrock Press.

Stix, A., & Hrbek, F. (2006). *Teachers and classroom coaches: How to motivate students across the content areas.* Alexandria, VA: Association for Supervision and Curriculum Development.

Sutyak, J., Lebeau, R., & O'Donnell, A. (1998). Unstructured cases in case-based learning benefit students with primary care career preferences. *American Journal of Surgery, 175,* 503–507.

Trilling, B., & Fadel, C. (2009). *21st-century skills: Learning for life in our times.* Hoboken, NJ: Jossey-Bass.

Wagner, T. (2008). *The global achievement gap: Why even our best schools don't teach the new survival skills our children need—and what we can do about it.* New York, NY: Basic Books.

Webb, N. L. (2005). *Web Alignment Tool (WAT) training manual, draft version 1.1 .* Madison, WI: Wisconsin Center for Education Research. Retrieved from http://wat.wceruw.org/Training%20Manual%202.1%20Draft%2009091205.doc

Weimer, M. (2012). Six paths to more authentic teaching. *Faculty Focus.* Retrieved from https://www.facultyfocus.com/articles/faculty-development/six-paths-to-more-authentic-teaching

Weinstock, M. B., & Klauer, K. M. (2011). *Bouncebacks! Medical and legal.* Columbus, OH: Anadem.

Wiggins, G., & McTighe, J. (2005). *Understanding by design* (2nd ed.). Alexandria, VA: Association for Supervision and Curriculum Development.

Williams, B. (2004). The implementation of case-based learning—Shaping the pedagogy in ambulance education. *Journal of Emergency Primary Health Care, 2* (3–4).

Windham, C. (2007). *Why today's students value authentic learning.* Educause Learning Initiative. Retrieved from https://www.educause.edu/ir/library/pdf/ELI3017.pdf

About the Author

Todd Stanley is the author of more than 12 teacher education books, including *Project-Based Learning for Gifted Students: A Handbook for the 21st-Century Classroom* and *Performance-Based Assessment for 21st-Century Skills*, as well as the 10 Performance-Based Projects series. He was a classroom teacher for 18 years, working with students as young as second graders and as old as high school seniors, and was a National Board Certified teacher. He helped create a gifted academy for grades 5–8, which employed inquiry-based learning, problem-based learning, project-based learning, case-based learning, and performance-based assessment. He is currently the gifted services coordinator for Pickerington Local School District in Ohio, where he lives with his wife, Nicki, and two daughters, Anna and Abby. You can follow him on Twitter @the_gifted_guy, where he posts photos and thoughts about many of the strategies discussed in this book.